mass career customization

mass career customization

ALIGNING THE WORKPLACE WITH
TODAY'S NONTRADITIONAL WORKFORCE

cathleen benko

anne weisberg

Harvard Business School Press

Boston, Massachusetts

Library of Congress Cataloging-in-Publication Data

Benko, Cathleen, 1958–
   Mass career customization : aligning the workplace with today's nontraditional workforce / Cathleen Benko, Anne Weisberg.
     p. cm.
   Includes index.
   ISBN-13: 978-1-4221-1033-1 (hardcover : alk. paper)
   ISBN-10: 1-4221-1033-8
    1. Organizational change. 2. Manpower planning. 3. Employee retention. 4. Career development. I. Weisberg, Anne C. (Anne Cicero) II. Title.
   HD58.8.B4588 2007
   658.3'128—dc22

                             2007009121

To those who create the future

CONTENTS

Acknowledgments   *ix*

1   From Ladder to Lattice   1

2   The Nontraditional Is the New Traditional   25

3   Why Flexible Work Arrangements
    Are Not the Answer   57

4   Mass Career Customization   77
    *The Framework for Aligning the Workplace
    with the Workforce*

5   The Journey Toward a Lattice Organization   109

6   Facing Forward   147
    Sage Advice from the Front Line, to the Front Line

7   Living in a Lattice World   167

Notes   *189*
Bibliography   *209*
Index   *219*
About the Authors   *229*

ACKNOWLEDGMENTS

Statesman and philosopher Cicero once said that "gratitude is not only the greatest of virtues, but the parent of all others." In our minds, that says it all. This book is a testament to the generosity of a plethora of individuals who opened up their schedules and their lives to candidly share their experiences, observations, stories, and insights. This work is so much richer for their contributions.

We are grateful for a remarkable leadership team, particularly Sharon Allen, Jim Quigley, and Barry Salzberg, who, when presented with a whole new way to view workforce, talent, and careers—and the relationship of these with the workplace—embraced the notion in "Why not?" fashion. Their support and conviction have been absolute and unwavering. Similarly, we are grateful to our colleagues, who, both directly and indirectly, influenced this effort in countless ways. Partnership works, and the whole is surely greater than the sum of any individual's knowledge and experience.

We are also humbled by the many people in our everyday lives who contributed in a multitude of ways, from picking up the slack in our day jobs; to offering to take our kids for the day; to responding to requests that, however nominal (or not), received that extra attention. We sense, through these considerate acts, that others see the potential and magnitude of this work. We're awed by each of you for who you are and how you extend yourselves for others.

Any project of this kind ultimately comes down to hard work. Tom Hayes and Jenna Carl were an integral part of bringing this book to fruition, as were our WIN team, our friends at Volume, Jackie Boyle, Molly Anderson, and Steve Riordan, who in various ways added immeasurably to the final product.

Finally, well, there's no place like home. We're blessed to be surrounded by encouraging and supportive families. To George, Brendan, Ellie, PD, Rachie, Matthew, Sarah, Margaret, Elena, and Elizabeth, we trust that this work reflects all you have showed us about how to make the most of any journey.

ONE

From Ladder to Lattice

*They always say time changes things, but you
actually have to change them yourself.*

—Andy Warhol

Scaling the corporate ladder has been the enduring gold standard for personal success since organizational hierarchy was invented two centuries ago at the beginning of the industrial age. But organizational hierarchy is not what it used to be. Neither is the corporate ladder—nor the corporate workforce.

A confluence of market and demographic forces in the past twenty years has compressed hierarchies, shortened the ladder, and reduced the qualified pool of high-potential employees available to climb it. Another set of business and societal influences has reshaped the American workforce in gender mix and diversity. Employees' views and experiences have changed markedly regarding what constitutes the "normal" good life.

Only 17 percent of households now have a husband in the workforce and a wife who is not, down from 63 percent in 1950 when the first baby boomers were not even in kindergarten. With 83 percent of U.S. households now considered "nontraditional," there's little wonder why many executives are either sensing or already confronting mounting tensions.

These tensions are rooted in the misalignment between the traditional workplace and the largely nontraditional workforce and in the stunning transformation of an economy dominated increasingly by knowledge-driven services. Such changes have placed huge demands for rapid adjustments on employers and employees—all within the amazingly brief span of just two generations.

The urgent question, then, is how should business leaders realign their workplace norms and practices with the realities of today's nontraditional workforce? The answer, in short, is by adopting the framework of *mass career customization* (MCC)™.

MCC is centered on the powerful insight that the career journey in the knowledge-driven economy will increasingly look like a sine wave of sorts, an undulating wave of climbing and falling phases over time. As the working population shrinks, maintaining industry advantage will depend largely on keeping employees engaged and connected. MCC provides a framework for organizational adaptability that will do just that.

MCC provides a structure, systematic approach, and corporate lexicon that allows organizations to correlate employees' talents, career aspirations, and evolving life circumstances over time in ways that match up with the enterprise's evolving marketplace strategies and commensurate need for talent. Equally important, MCC recognizes, validates, and embraces the changing tempos of today's knowledge workers, offering a scalable solution to the enervating dilemmas in their search for career-life integration.

In this way, MCC does for careers what mass product customization (MPC) has done for the consumer products industry: replace a one-size-fits-all approach with a bevy of customized product offerings. The results of MPC? Higher profits, lower costs, and greater satisfaction for customers and loyalty for producers.

Similarly, MCC delivers distinct competitive advantage through increased employee job satisfaction and loyalty; greater potential for the kinds of continuous, long-term relationships with higher-performing employees that improves productivity; and lower costs related to less employee churn.

THE NEW WORKFORCE IMPERATIVE

MCC is the framework that presents a structured response to the demise of the corporate ladder and the rise of a more adaptive model of career progression that we term the *corporate lattice*. Our inspiration for this name comes from the realm of mathematics. In mathematics, a lattice ladder allows one to move in many directions between a set and its subsets and is not limited to upward or downward progress.[1] Lattices also are structures that can be repeated infinitely at any scale in the theoretical world.

In the real world, lattices are common features in everyday environments from rose gardens to ivy walls. They are living platforms for growth, with upward momentum visible along the many paths, twists, and turns toward the top. In this way, lattices are more varied than ladders, which provide a more singular upward path of unalterable steps (see figure 1-1).

MCC enables the transition from corporate ladder to corporate lattice that we see emerging in large enterprises by giving employees and managers a scalable, transparent context for customizing careers. From the enterprise's perspective, MCC is a

FIGURE 1-1

Ladder versus lattice

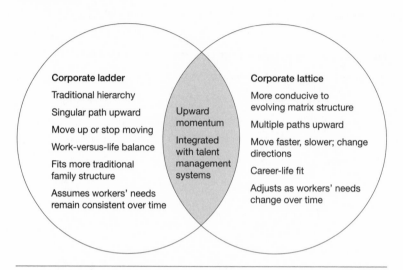

pragmatic new way to keep pace with market growth, attract and retain valued employees, and strengthen the leadership pipeline. From the employee's perspective, a corporate lattice metaphor and notion of customizing careers creates alternatives to the all-or-nothing decisions many employees, historically women, continue to confront at various stages in their careers.

The need for these alternatives in today's workplace is urgent. Long before they enter the workforce, women, in particular, talk openly with friends about how they will decide career and family priorities. They anticipate that very appealing job promotion offers will arrive a few years into their careers in corporations or professional services firms—and that the timing of these offers will collide with their biological clocks. The nightmare of these younger women is being trapped in a workforce model dominated by the corporate ladder, with little option except to move up or step off.

Women's struggles with career-family issues are employers' struggles, too. More than half of all management jobs are now held by women, and nearly 60 percent of all college and graduate students are women.[2] Yet women are not the only ones with anxiety about future trade-offs. Many men in Generations X and Y, ranging in age now from their late teens to early forties, say they are less inclined than boomers to compete on the corporate ladder if the cost to their family and personal lives is too high.[3] They insist on meaningful work *and* meaningful personal lives.[4]

The choices among these trade-offs are particularly stressful when employees are starting families, a rite of passage in high gear now for many men and women in Generation X and soon to be engaged by Generation Y. Sorting through the fallout of these career-life trade-offs among employees often is stressful for the enterprise as well: many of these employees receive expensive training and other investments to develop them as key players, network contributors, and prospective leaders. Those retained at this crucial point in their personal lives are more likely to remain loyal; those who leave usually are lost for good.

WHY HERE AND WHY NOW

So why is here and now the time to acknowledge and respond to the notion that our corporate structures are morphing from a ladder to a lattice construct? One reason is that six key trends, each of which is likely familiar to us, are converging in ways that create an unprecedented workforce challenge for business executives (see the box "Six Converging Workforce Trends"). These trends have been observable for years, in some cases decades, but as they converge, their momentum is accelerating and compounding in part because other factors that had offset the impact of these trends

Six Converging Workforce Trends

- Shrinking pool of skilled labor
- Changing family structures
- Increasing number of women
- Changing expectations of men
- Emerging expectations of Generations X and Y
- Increasing impact of technology

are now waning. The high rate of immigration pre-9/11 is one such example of a condition that masked underlying trends.[5]

The result is creating sweeping dislocations in workforce composition, attitudes, and capabilities. Most can sense today that something is afoot. Part of our aim is to put the situation in context, making it more tangible and therefore easier to address.

We explore the details and implications of these trends broadly in chapter 2, but note here a few key findings from recent studies that underscore the growing strategic significance of today's workforce challenge. First, given recent and projected birthrates and anticipated rates of immigration, the U.S. workforce is projected to grow only 4 percent between 2010 and 2020 and a meager 3 percent from 2020 to 2030, compared with 12 percent in this decade. These statistics equate to an anemic annual growth rate of 0.3 percent by 2020, compared with more than 1 percent today.[6] This estimate incorporates current projections for rising immigration and offshore outsourcing to India, China, and elsewhere.

Women's representation in the labor force, on the other hand, continues to increase. Women have been the canary in the corporate coal mine for more than twenty-five years, struggling to blend career and family life, sometimes successfully negotiating their own one-off arrangements and sometimes opting out in frustration.[7] Many researchers point to the 1970s as the period when conventional standards and assumptions about the time and location of how work was conducted began to break down. That was also when women in general and women with children in particular became increasingly more prevalent at work. Today they are entrenched as vital contributors and, increasingly, leaders throughout the resurgent U.S. economy.

More recently, research studies involving men, particularly those of Generations X and Y, show they too are increasingly dissatisfied with managers' expectations for rigid time-and-place execution of work requirements.[8] Relatively few of them believe they even have permission to discuss trade-offs and potential adjustments between career and family life.[9] However, James J. Sandman, managing partner from 1995 to 2005 at Arnold & Porter, a major law firm based in Washington, D.C., says men leaving the firm in recent years have become increasingly vocal in citing their need for more family and personal time as a major motivator in rejecting a future in large-firm law practice. "This is a much larger issue than a women's issue," he said.[10]

In fact, men have become worse off than women in many ways in searching for solutions. They fear that merely raising the subject will cause them to be viewed as less committed, relegated to less appealing work, or worse yet, shunned or put out to pasture. Yet the American workplace today, perhaps 90 percent or more of it, remains largely calibrated to family patterns and life cycle rhythms of the early- and mid-twentieth century, when wives typically raised children at home and husbands worked forty hours a week in a factory, office, or store. We have reached an inflection point for managing the enterprise workplace. Yes, the time has come for these antiquated standards to change.

MASS CAREER CUSTOMIZATION: THE EMERGING STANDARD

More specifically, the relationship between employer and employee needs to shift from an implicit and fairly rigid contract toward more transparent, continuous collaboration. The MCC framework is the emerging standard for aligning current and future career development options for the employee with current and future requirements of the business in ways that are sustainable for both.

The principles of MCC include:

- Increasing choices that help employees shape career paths that fit the various stages of their personal lives

- Making career building a more explicitly shared responsibility between the enterprise and the individual

- Making adaptability over time a core competency for individuals and enterprises

- Creating transparency regarding trade-offs and choices that lead to better planning, better decisions, and greater satisfaction

- Selecting choices that are good for both the employee and the enterprise

- Retaining talent by cultivating a new sense of loyalty and connection

As consumers, we have become very used to expecting manufacturers and retailers to customize all sorts of things in our daily lives—personal computers, denim jeans, sneakers, credit card billing cycles, and so on. Why not extend this popular and profitable concept of defined choices in the consumer marketplace to the workplace?

Customizing careers within a corporate lattice construct can benefit employees and organizations in countless ways, in contrast to the limited options in corporate-ladder organizations. For example, one growing concern of Generations X and Y is that large numbers of the boomer generation will *not* retire, essentially forming a "gray ceiling" that will take these rising generations still more years to penetrate within traditional corporate-ladder organizations.[11] The corporate lattice allows both younger and older generations to contribute and continue to develop along many pathways. Women with years of experience within an organization can stay in the system, without having to drop out, even if they have periods when their family obligations constrain their contributions at work.

Applying the latticelike framework of MCC presents new opportunities to attract, retain, and cultivate long-term loyalty for younger employees who likely will want to accelerate and decelerate at different stages in their careers. At the same time, the lattice creates more options for empty nesters who can now devote greater time to their employers as well as for aging boomers who may want to downshift at a pace that fits their personal lives, instead of being forced into the all-or-nothing decision to stay longer than they want in roles demanding full-throttle commitment.

Enterprise leaders who recognize how the six trends are reshaping their workforce and can adapt accordingly will be better able to keep pace with emerging, effective responses. Those who can execute extraordinarily well in these adjustments, and remain committed to them, can even create opportunities for significant competitive advantage.

Some companies have been successful in responding to one or two of these six trends without requiring a significant transformation of their employment or workplace policies and practices—that is, their human capital systems. But they will have to be more pro-active and inventive going forward. To catch up and keep pace with the new workforce, enterprises need to rethink the workplace, transforming their personnel systems, organizational structures, and cultures (and attitudes) to support their high-performing and high-potential employees, in customizing careers.

We believe countless high-performing, high-potential employees who opted out of their enterprises or in other ways underperformed relative to their potential in recent decades could have been retained if the customized career option had been visible and viable as they weighed these difficult choices. A landmark study by Professor Myra M. Hart hints at the magnitude of the resulting losses to business and the economy. Her analysis indicated that 62 percent of Harvard Business School's women graduates with more than one child were either not working or working part-time five years or more after graduation.[12] A similar study of 1970-or-later graduates of the Stanford Graduate School of Business showed that 35 percent of women had a career break of at least one year, and 64 percent said it was for family reasons.[13]

The multipath options possible through the application of career customization principles cannot be negotiated by employees in the more unyielding, one-size-fits-all tradition of the corporate-ladder approach and attitudes toward career development. Some one-off deals, designed as accommodations to the traditional path, have worked while as many have seemed to fail, resulting in the employee having to step off the ladder.[14] Others have had to step off without even the option of a one-off deal.

Our initial experience in putting the framework and processes of MCC into action strongly suggests this approach is far more appealing to employees than the common benefit now available to accommodate circumstances in their family and personal lives: the flexible work arrangement.

FLEXIBLE WORK ARRANGEMENTS:
ADMIRABLE—BUT NOT THE ANSWER

In the 1980s, many companies began, somewhat begrudgingly, to introduce policies that recognized the growing employees' demand for options to address child care and other family responsibilities along with their work requirements. Again, these changes were initiated primarily by women. The first steps into flextime often included maternity leave and flexible work schedules. These and similar accommodations have since blossomed to be referred to as "flexible work arrangements" (FWAs).

In the 1990s, formal FWAs were adopted more widely as companies increasingly recognized their importance for recruiting and retaining high-performing employees.[15] Yet these have shown a mixed response, at best, considering that women over thirty with children had entered the workforce by the millions beginning in the 1970s and that, still today, high-potential, high-talent women cite work-life conflict as a top factor in why they leave their companies. Charles Rodgers, a pioneer in advocating more options in the workplace for employees, reported in a 1992 study of more than twenty large corporations that despite "enormous demand" in the workforce, fewer than a third of employees had access to formal flextime.[16]

"The interest in more flexible work practices stems from the tremendous time constraints faced by many employees with significant family responsibilities," Rodgers said. "Current practices, schedules and management philosophy are no longer adequate for workers in this important segment of the labor force and impede them from being as productive as they could be."[17]

As we explore more extensively in chapter 3, recent research shows wider availability of FWAs but at the same time suggests relatively little else has changed.[18] These FWAs focus primarily on maternity leaves and part-time scheduling related to childbirth, child rearing, and, increasingly, elder care. Many employees believe that pursuing an FWA for this and other reasons will be perceived by colleagues and managers as a lack of commitment. Moreover, men perceive FWAs as an option for women only, a perception that indeed reflects the reality of FWA activity in most companies. Women, particularly working mothers, still represent the vast majority of employees who take advantage of FWAs.[19]

Many managers regard FWAs as, at best, a business inconvenience to accommodate a worker and, at worst, an irritation to achieving business objectives—*their* business objectives. The tradeoffs are unclear and often unspoken. When negotiating an FWA, managers and employees often fail to address the impact on compensation, advancement, and performance expectations, which leads to mismatched expectations. FWAs, although formally a contract between an employee and supervisor, informally affect all team or department members whose roles are linked to this employee's activities and responsibilities. Some coworkers feel they continually need to "pick up the slack," while customers may feel inconvenienced or poorly served due to the limited availability of an account representative on an FWA.

Moreover, FWAs are considered costly to the enterprise broadly and to the supervisor directly in part because they cannot be scaled. FWAs must be negotiated on a case-by-case basis between the supervisor and the employee with little structure or policy to support these discussions. FWAs also are consuming more of supervisors' time, which you may be experiencing yourself, as requests for FWAs proliferate and soon are expected to reach critical mass. Both the scale and critical mass issues are additional factors creating new urgency in the "why here and why now" discussion. For these reasons, many managers regard FWAs as compromises to their expectation that full-time employees under their supervision will do what it takes to climb the corporate ladder.

Many *Fortune* 500 companies and leading professional services firms have offered FWAs in various forms for the past ten years or more, some even touting these arrangements in their recruiting collateral. The evidence is clear, though, that this benefit has not succeeded in helping employers retain vast numbers of workers. Why is this the case? FWAs have significant limitations because they typically:

- Are point solutions addressing only the hours and location of work at a specific time in an employee's work life

- Are often limited to lower-level staff positions, which are far fewer in number than the line positions through which most business activities are directly transacted

- Do not anticipate changing family and personal commitments—increasing *and* decreasing—outside of work throughout a career

- Do not include longer-term planning for an employee's career progression in roles, quality of assignments, pace for promotions, and responsibilities

The unintended consequences of these failings are that FWAs sharply limit the potential career growth of the employees who require their immediate or short-term benefits. For these very reasons, the FWA limitations discourage employees with career ambitions. Four in ten women with children, for example, leave the workforce, primarily for family reasons, at some point in their careers.[20]

Even so, the volume of one-off negotiations over how and when work gets done has expanded sharply as more and more men and women are demanding that their employers respond to their needs.[21] Managers need a framework that is scalable, provides policy boundaries, and works within the context of a career—rather than a point solution—to help them operate more comfortably in what inevitably are highly personal discussions.

CREATING THE NEW NORMAL

Mass career customization provides both scalability and policy boundaries, as well as the transparency and consistency lacking in FWAs, that enable managers to communicate more effectively with employees about career plans.

A conceptual cousin to the successful marketing and manufacturing of customized consumer products, MCC is a natural evolution from the traditional corporate-ladder path, with its one-size-fits-all approach, and the one-off FWA approach of accommodation through point solutions. MCC is a framework that helps enterprises promote multidimensional, customized career experiences. The payback is a more actively engaged and loyal workforce.

We describe the core elements of MCC, how they work in relation to each other, and how they holistically support an individual's career planning and progression in chapters 4–6. The brief explanation and narrative that follows in this chapter is intended simply as an introduction to the four main dimensions of a career and how choices among them provide real options to individualize careers.

MCC assumes a definite, not infinite, set of options along four career dimensions—Pace, Workload, Location/Schedule, and Role—and provides a structure to manage these options as commonplace events, rather than one-off accommodations. Employees customize their careers by selecting, in counsel with their managers, the option within each of the dimensions that most closely matches their career objectives, taking into account their life circumstances, at that interval of time. (These options are revisited periodically as circumstances evolve.) Visual representation provided through individualized profiles helps both employees and managers clarify expectations for specific work contributions, evaluations, and associated rewards.

Figure 1-2 illustrates a typical MCC profile for a midcareer sales manager. The setting in the Pace dimension is near the center of the continuum, indicating he is on a midrange track toward promotion, with increasing authority and responsibility. He is working full-time with no restrictions, meaning he travels whenever necessary and without any limit on work location. (In other words, Workload is recorded at the "full" level, and Location/Schedule is set at "not restricted.") The setting for Role, several nodes down the continuum, signals he is a midlevel manager.

The MCC profile provides a snapshot of a person's career at a given point in time but is also designed to be adjusted over time. MCC provides a wide range of options for creating careers that suit employees' needs today, while looking ahead to future circumstances and priorities they may be anticipating. Typical examples include starting a family, pursuing advanced educational opportunities, or wanting to accelerate to attain a professional goal more expeditiously than those on a normal track.

FIGURE 1-2

A common MCC employee profile

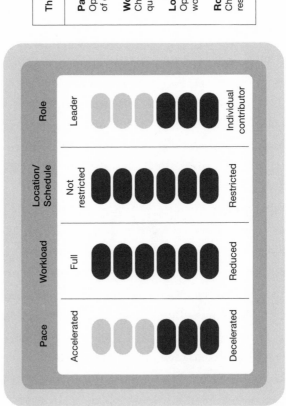

	Pace	Workload	Location/Schedule	Role
Top	Accelerated	Full	Not restricted	Leader
Bottom	Decelerated	Reduced	Restricted	Individual contributor

The four dimensions of MCC

Pace
Options relating to the rate of career progression

Workload
Choices relating to the quantity of work output

Location/Schedule
Options for when and where work is performed

Role
Choices in position and responsibilities

Elements of informal MCC are happening everywhere, albeit in varieties of one-off manifestations. Individuals work from home one or two days a week (Location/Schedule) or turn down a promotion (Pace) so that they can have the time to care for elderly parents. Parents of young children shift from line to staff roles to limit travel (Role) or reduce the number of hours worked each week to fit in their myriad responsibilities (Workload). And so on.

IT'S ALREADY GOING ON

From what we have observed, many cases of informal MCC appear at first to be characterized by an unusually well-managed, holistic sequence of FWAs. In retrospect, however, these success stories often are revealed as felicitous seat-of-the-pants progressions that happened to work out well. Only a few individuals are able to navigate multiple steps off and back on either a career ladder or informal lattice over the years.

The following example of one employee, Tina, is a good illustration of how informal MCC occurs in many enterprises. (Additional examples of informal MCC are examined in chapter 5.) Tina's case is typical in marking a progression of one-off FWA negotiations that happened to work out well and, indeed, include several features of the MCC framework. That said, it is a look back through the rear-view mirror of a best-case FWA scenario, not an illustration of the road we envision ahead.

Figure 1-3 illustrates how Tina's career progression would have been recorded, in five different stages, if it had been managed through the MCC framework. Each of the five profiles represents a separate stage expressed along the four dimensions. The continuum in Workload, for example, varies in the five profiles from as

FIGURE 1-3

Tina's MCC profile stages

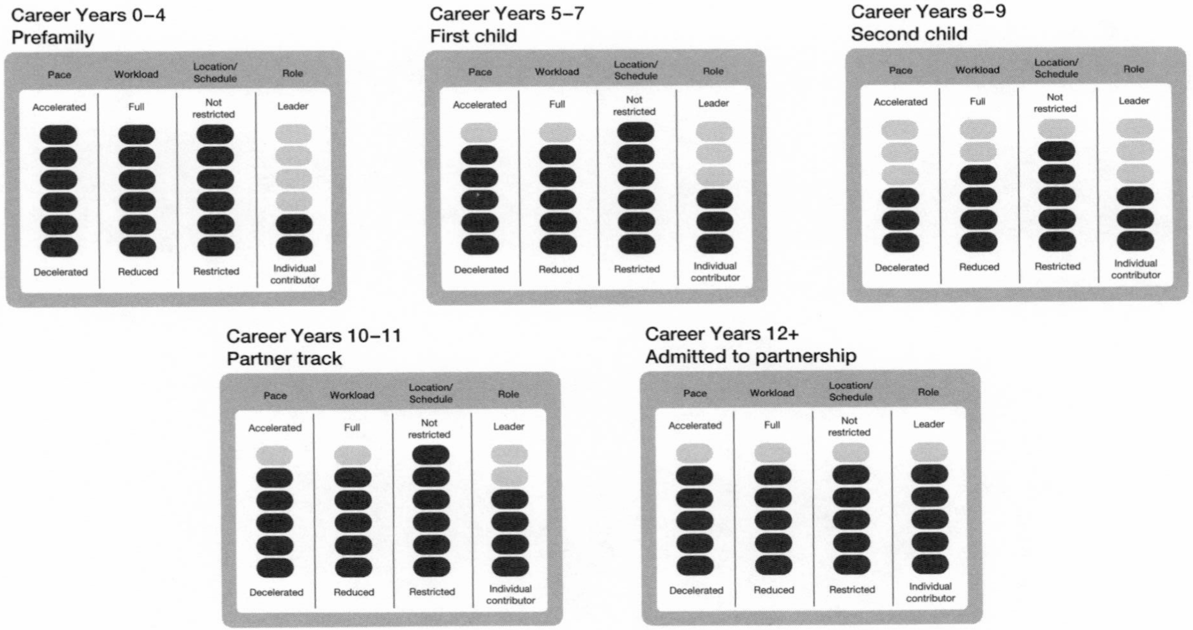

Career Years 0–4
Prefamily

Career Years 5–7
First child

Career Years 8–9
Second child

Career Years 10–11
Partner track

Career Years 12+
Admitted to partnership

high as full in the prefamily stage to as low as three nodes in the second-child stage.

The key point here is to recognize how certain nodes on the vertical dimensions change from one stage to the next as Tina's work profile evolves to keep pace with varying events in her personal life. In Career Years 0–4, Tina is hired by the audit staff and "dials up" to the highest level on three of the four work dimensions. Staffed on a high-profile client engagement, she performs well and impresses her managers. Fours years later, after a fast-track promotion to audit manager, she takes a three-month leave of absence when her first child is born. She returns with a 90 percent Workload, remains at that level for three years (Career Years 5–7), and then shortly after promotion to senior manager, takes a six-month leave for the birth of her second child.

She returns from the leave to a 70 percent Workload (to preserve additional family time) and reassigns herself from a prestigious client to a smaller project (Career Years 8–9). This new assignment introduces her to different partners who, over time, become key players in advancing her career.

She dials up to 85 percent in Workload (Career Years 10–11), continuing her audit role and adding leadership activities to advance her candidacy for partner. In her eleventh year, she becomes a partner. In the next year, she maintains her slightly "dialed-down" Workload and shifts to a moderately flexible schedule that fits seasonal audit demands and more immediate client projects and consultations (Career Years 12+).

Think of Tina's career journey to date as a pseudo–sine wave with rising and falling phases along a baseline, which over time rises steadily as she advances in her personally calibrated blend of career and family life. This process—negotiated and navigated by Tina and her supervisors over more than a decade—enabled her to expand her professional skills and experience at a pace that meshed well with her family priorities. She also established a foundation for thirty years or more of future professional growth and rewards.

Her employer wins by retaining her direct contributions and knowledge capital; saving the cost of attracting, recruiting, and training another who might well experience the same issues down the road; and building loyalty in a scarce skills market.

MANAGING TRADE-OFFS

We know that many executives and managers will voice serious doubts initially about implementing mass career customization. What if the floodgates open and too many people opt for part-time schedules? Or if too many choose no-travel provisions, or no assignments on Mondays or Tuesdays? Managers might raise these and other concerns and conclude that they won't be able to fulfill their business needs.

A series of MCC pilot programs, the first initiated in 2005, proves these fears to be off the mark (see chapter 5). The surprising choice turned out to be just the opposite of many managers' fears: a large number of employees said they wanted to dial *up*, especially in Pace and Workload. They wanted to advance further and faster, especially employees under thirty years old.

Many signs of these differing generational attitudes and ambitions abound. A Generation X cofounder of a real estate investment firm and onetime Bank of America employee told *Fortune* magazine, "My father was a loyal corporate soldier who worked at the same company for 32 years . . . But my generation is more interested in opportunities for fast growth than in security."[22]

Accommodating a surge in dial-up choices requires managers to make adjustments to staffing and promotion models, just as they must do with dial-down choices. For employees, when the number of hours worked is dialed down, compensation will be reduced as well. As fewer hours result in reduced work contributions, their pace toward the next promotion is slowed. In these cases managers must learn to separate the *quality* of employees' work from the *quantity* of their work in grading their performance both on absolute and relative scales.

These and other trade-offs are essential parts of the MCC process. They must factor into every employee's analysis of specific choices across the four career dimensions that will best fit his or her career planning. Trade-offs also should be part of regular discussions between counselors and employees. Training supervisors, counselors, and employees on how to manage and engage in these conversations is part of the transformation required to create an MCC-enabled organization.

To be sure, companies with excellent reputations for their workforce dynamics have embraced and delivered for many years on some of the elements in mass career customization. Lockheed Martin, for one, rotates high-potential employees through positions as a way of exposing them to more career options and future opportunities—which creates more role options. The company also requires more experienced managers in the boomer generation to mentor and advise younger employees on career planning. Since 2001, turnover at the company has averaged 2.5 percent, far below the double-digit levels that are the norm among many of its competitors.[23]

"Recruiters try to woo you by offering you more money, but it's really about a combination of things this company does, especially the emphasis on learning," said Ngina McLean, a thirty-one-year-old systems engineering manager. "It's the only place I've worked where I can see spending my whole career."[24] With testimonials like that, it is no surprise that Lockheed Martin ranked in the top three, along with the Walt Disney Company and Deloitte, in a 2006 *BusinessWeek*-sponsored survey of the "50 best places" for college graduates to start a career.[25]

THE OPTION VALUE OF MCC

With the MCC framework, employees, together with their employers, can discover abundant options to design and achieve what they consider to be their optimal career paths—whether or not they ever need or choose to take advantage of these options. Knowing this is possible and seeing how others are pursuing their own objectives will be a strong inducement for employees to stay connected in a continuous relationship—and for sought-after recruits to sign on at the start of their careers.

Many employees and recruits who see no evidence that they can customize career choices at pivotal stages of their personal and business careers instinctively look for other career opportunities where they are more likely to have those choices. This happens even when employees are highly satisfied with their current job situations and the next pivotal stage in their careers is several years away.

Solving the misalignment between the workplace, today's system of work, and the new realities of family, household, and generational patterns and structures in today's nontraditional workforce is an urgent priority for all C-level executives. The corporate-lattice organization, grounded in the MCC framework and options, is a comprehensive solution to this misalignment for the employee and the enterprise. The processes deliver both immediate options and far-sighted planning. They encourage employees—especially those identified as highly valued for future business success—to remain loyal and connected.

For the enterprise, improving employee retention strengthens competitiveness through significant savings in the HR and operational budgets. By contributing directly to workforce stability, a high rate of employee retention is also fundamental for improving customer service, customer retention, and, ultimately, revenues. Annual employee turnover exceeds 15 percent in many industries, so recruitment costs can be especially staggering for fast-growth businesses. Most workforce experts agree that the costs to attract, train, and retain a new employee with experience and skills similar to those of the one being replaced is, conservatively, at least twice the former employee's average salary. These costs range as high as five times the former employee's annual salary in organizations that compete primarily on the knowledge and analytical skills of their employees.

Solving the "my life doesn't fit into my work and my work doesn't fit into my life" conundrum is a lofty goal for both employer and employee. But as you'll see through the remainder of this book, MCC offers a compelling answer—for both employer *and* employee.

TWO

The Nontraditional Is the New Traditional

All is flux; nothing stays still.

—Heraclitus

It seems that every day another news story appears about the changing workforce.[1] Headlines range from the *Economist*'s cover story "The Search for Talent: Why It's Getting Harder to Find" to *Fortune*'s cover story "Get A Life! Ditching the 24/7 Culture" to the *New York Times*' "When Work Time Isn't Face Time."[2] The media's attention is indicative of the growing importance of these issues to society and, therefore, to business leaders. Yet historical workforce trends are still by and large treated as disparate and disconnected. What do working mothers have in common with members of Generation Y, who appear more concerned about their social lives than their working lives? What do stagnating college graduation rates have to do with the yearnings for "having a life" expressed by more and more men?

In this chapter, we dissect the six key trends (see figure 2-1) and illustrate how each is exacerbating the friction between workforce challenges and structural workplace impediments. To be sure, some companies have successfully addressed one or two of these trends without having to redesign their core career-ladder systems and processes. But the *convergence* of these trends is forcing companies to respond to the requirements and expectations of the knowledge-driven workforce by creating new approaches for how work gets done and careers are built.

FIGURE 2-1

The convergence of six key trends impacting the workforce

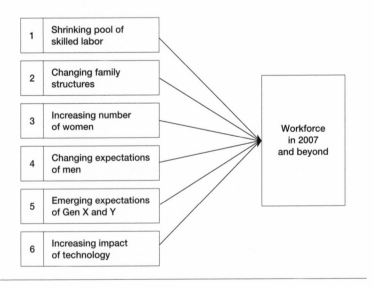

TREND 1: THE SHORTAGE OF SKILLED KNOWLEDGE ECONOMY WORKERS

Over the next ten years, we can expect increasing shortages of the labor you desire most. This will be a function of (1) retiring baby boomers; (2) lower birthrates; (3) increased competition for skilled workers around the globe; (4) stagnant college graduation rates relative to rising demand for well-educated knowledge workers; and (5) declining competency in basic skills such as writing and math by high school students and even college graduates.

While the knowledge economy demands employees who are well educated with competent communication and analytic skills, these employees are in short supply today—and this shortage will only get worse over the next ten years. The Employment Policy Foundation estimates that by 2012 there will be a *6 million person* gap in this country between the number of students graduating from college and the number of workers needed to cover job growth and replace retirees.

Some industries and sectors are already experiencing this skills gap.[3] According to NASA projections, "U.S. colleges will graduate only 198,000 students [in science and engineering] to fill the shoes of 2 million boomers scheduled to retire between 1998 and 2008."[4] While the skills required to keep pace and succeed in a knowledge-based economy increase steadily, a 2006 survey of 431 business leaders describes new entrants into the workforce as lacking basic writing skills, including spelling and grammar, and basic math.[5] A third of these leaders "doubted their college graduate employees could write a simple business letter."[6]

However, even if businesses can upgrade the skills of the people they are hiring, there are fewer and fewer people entering the workforce. The boomer generation, at about 80 million people, is almost twice the size of the generation behind it, Generation X, at about 46 million people. Generation Y comprises about 76 million people and is only now starting to enter the workforce. Together, the boomers and Gen Y are creating an hourglass effect with the greatest number of workers at opposite ends of the career spectrum (see figure 2-2).

Getting past the shrinking pool of experienced, skilled workers over the next decade is just one factor to consider. There are others. For instance, when experienced managers move on, the intellectual and social capital they have accumulated within their organizations and across their industries' ecosystems leave with them. Transferring this knowledge to those employees rising behind

FIGURE 2-2

Numeric change in labor force by age, projected 2004–2014 (in thousands)

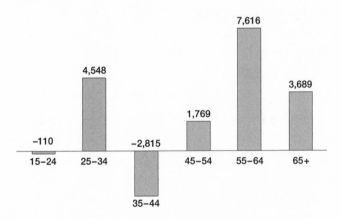

Source: U.S. Bureau of Labor, "Labor Force," *Occupational Outlook Quarterly* 49, no. 4 (Winter 2005–2006): 46–53.

them is critical. It is also why retaining emerging, experienced, and committed leaders is a strategic necessity now more than ever.

Second, births are barely at replacement rates today in this country. Essentially, the U.S. workforce will stop growing. As summarized by authors Ken Dychtwald, Tamara J. Erickson, and Robert Morison in their book *Workforce Crisis: How to Beat the Coming Shortage of Skills and Talent*: "[T]he *rate* of growth [of the workforce] will decline from 12 percent this decade to only 4 percent between 2010 and 2020, then 3 percent between 2020 and 2030. This translates into a drop from today's annual growth rate of just over 1 percent to an anemic 0.3 percent by around 2020."[7]

While many companies assume that they will be able to fill the ranks with workers from overseas, the truth is that the U.S. birthrate is the envy of many nations, especially those in Europe that are already experiencing negative birthrates. News reports of unskilled labor shortages in China's manufacturing industries and studies noting talent shortfalls in its knowledge-driven export services sector are already starting to appear.[8] Among the world's largest economies, only India is projected to have a growth rate in working-age population higher than the United States and Mexico through 2050 (for the projected change in the working populations, see figure 2-3).

Moreover, immigration of skilled workers into the United States is waning due to policy and security changes and improved opportunities in foreign labor markets.[9] In recent years, immigration rates have leveled off in large part because the U.S. government reduced the number of visas offered annually by two-thirds. Moreover, post-9/11 security measures make getting a visa a more difficult and lengthier process, which further discourages applicants.[10] Talented foreign workers are increasingly inclined to stay

FIGURE 2-3

Projected change in the working-age population (15–64), 1970–2010 and 2010–2050

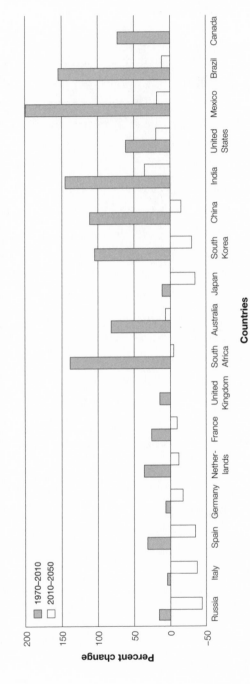

Source: Deloitte Research, "It's 2008: Do You Know Where Your Talent Is?" (New York: Deloitte Development LLC, 2004).

in their home markets as attractive new job opportunities, largely linked to the global economy, expand.

Fast-growing markets for skilled employees, such as those in India and China, are becoming more and more attractive to highly educated workers—they no longer have to leave their home countries to find high-level career opportunities.[11] Microsoft Chairman Bill Gates says his company's R&D centers in India and China are teeming with highly educated Indian and Chinese nationals, respectively, "most of who, historically, would have come to the United States." Now, he adds, "[M]ore are either not coming at all, or coming here and then going back."[12]

Nearly two decades ago, workforce visionary Felice N. Schwartz anticipated a future that is arriving now with remarkable accuracy and immediacy. Several societal and technological trends that she identified have begun to alter the competitive balance across all businesses and industries. "If future population remains fairly stable while the economy continues to expand," Schwartz concluded in 1989, "and if the new information society simultaneously creates a greater need for creative, educated managers, then the gap between supply and demand will grow dramatically, and with it, the competition for managerial talent."[13]

This growing scarcity of talent will amplify the challenges of recruiting and retaining knowledgeable workers. Given this trend and those to follow, a key component of any talent strategy will be addressing the increasing demand for more elasticity in career paths.

TREND 2: CHANGES ON THE HOME FRONT

Scholars call it the "end of the lockstep lifestyle," an apt phrase for summing up the impact of tectonic shifts not only in career paths but also in the core social and family structures that have been taking place in the United States over the past thirty years.[14] "Today . . . there is no 'normal' life path," according to sociologist Phyllis Moen and psychologist Patricia Roehling, authors of *The Career Mystique: Cracks in the American Dream.* "Americans marry later or not at all, postpone parenthood, have fewer children (or none at all), move in and out of jobs, in and out of schooling, in and out of marriage or partnerships, and in and out of retirement."[15]

This increasingly diverse landscape of household profiles (see figure 2-4) is beginning to put pressure on workplace systems. On the whole, these systems were structured to match the mainstream rhythms of early- and mid-twentieth-century life, when

FIGURE 2-4

Changing family structures, 1950–2005

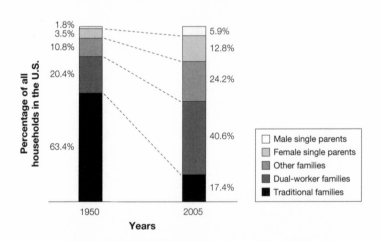

Source: Catalyst, *Two Careers, One Marriage: Making It Work in the Workplace* (New York: Catalyst, 1998). With updated data for 2005 from U.S. Bureau of Labor Statistics, *Annual Social and Economic Supplement: Current Population Survey* (Washington, DC: GPO, 2005).

most workers lived in traditional two-parent, single-income households in which the husband went to work and the wife stayed
at home.

A number of distinct trends have emerged in U.S. family structures since the 1970s. They include (1) a decrease in the marriage
rate; (2) an increase in dual-career households (see the box "A Profile of Dual-Earner Couples"); (3) reduced or delayed childbirth
among married couples; and (4) an increase in the number of
single-parent families.[16] Collectively, these changes mean there
is no longer a "normal" household—even though the traditional
career path assumes that there is.

For the first time in this country, more women are living without a spouse than with one, representing a profound shift away
from the central role that marriage has played in women's lives.[17]
Single-parent households have grown from just over 5 percent in

A Profile of Dual-Earner Couples

Couples in which both partners work are:

- Highly mobile due to greater financial security
- Likely to take advantage of "career customizing"
- A subgroup of the most highly valued employees
- Seeking greater work-life balance
- Likely to value work for more than just compensation
- Constantly thinking about career choices and evaluating
  career options[a]

a. Catalyst, *Two Careers, One Marriage: Making It Work in the Workplace* (New York:
Catalyst, 1998).

1950 to close to 18 percent in 2005. Single parents have less of a support structure at home and therefore need more support from work to meet their responsibilities in both spheres. In 1950, there were approximately 8 million dual-earner married couples and 25 million married couples with male breadwinners. In 2005, these numbers were 31 million and 13 million, respectively.

Although dual-earner families now make up over 40 percent of all households, the higher up the corporate ladder you go, the more likely that women will be in dual-career families and men will not. In a study funded by twelve multinational companies that surveyed their executives, 74 percent of married women executives have spouses who work full-time while 75 percent of married men executives have spouses who stay home.[18] This is one reason why senior women feel the strain of the corporate ladder more heavily than senior men: they are much more likely to also be the primary caregiver at home.

However, even dual-career couples who are not at the top of their organizations feel the strain of the work-life mismatch—because both are working longer hours, with no corresponding drop in their responsibilities at home.[19] This is especially salient for dual-career couples with children. According to Families and Work Institute, which has tracked these families for more than twenty years, mothers still spend more time than fathers caring for children, though fathers have increased their time with children significantly. As a result, 31 percent of fathers in dual-career couples take time off from work to care for or spend time with their child today, compared with only 12 percent in 1977.[20] No wonder, then, that dual-earner couples have a strong interest in controlling how and when they work. In fact, according to a Catalyst study of dual-career couples, they are seeking ways to customize their careers (see figure 2-5).[21]

FIGURE 2-5

Most important characteristics of a customized career path

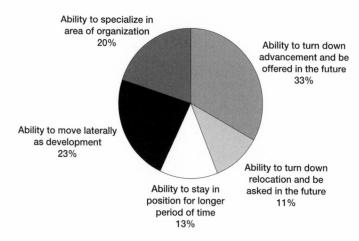

Source: Catalyst, *Two Careers, One Marriage: Making It Work in the Workplace* (New York: Catalyst, 1998).

Types of family responsibilities have evolved as well. Employees are increasingly spending time on elder care (see the box "Employees' Elder-Care Responsibilities"). As the boomer generation enters retirement, elder care will become a growing concern and responsibility for workers. Moreover, unlike child care, elder care can affect all workers, whether or not they have their own families, and impacts men and women equally.[22]

Each of these changes in family structures has consequences for the way men and women work and the way in which their careers play out. Fewer and fewer employees can focus solely on their professional lives because most do not have someone at home who can focus solely on personal and family matters.

The National Academy of Sciences has concluded that one of the main threats to remaining competitive in the science and

Employees' Elder-Care Responsibilities

Elder care is increasingly a responsibility of employees:

- Thirty-five percent of all men and women deal with elder care.[a]
- Ninety-two percent of organizations expect the number of employees caring for older relatives or friends to increase over the next five to ten years.[b] Indeed, 47 percent of organizations have seen an increase in employees' elder-care responsibilities.
- Sixty percent of organizations responded that employee expectations regarding elder-care issues have also increased in recent years.[c]

a. James T. Bond, Ellen Galinsky, Stacy S. Kim, Erin Brownfield, *2005 National Study of Employers: Highlight of Findings* (New York: Families and Work Institute, 2005), 3.
b. Society for Human Resource Management, *SHRM 2003 Eldercare Survey* (Alexandria, VA: Society of Human Resource Management Research, 2003).
c. Ibid.

engineering fields is "outmoded institutional structures" that assume the ability to devote oneself to work all the time, any time. "Anyone lacking the work and family support traditionally provided by a 'wife' is at a serious disadvantage in academe," the 2006 report said.[23] The report points to our concept of mass career customization as the way to replace the corporate ladder, epitomized in academia by the tenure track, with the varied-path approach of a corporate lattice.

TREND 3: INCREASING NUMBER OF WOMEN

Women are entering the workforce with better educations and, in turn, are better prepared to contribute rapidly and over the long term in knowledge-driven organizations. They are unquestionably a major source of talent for the foreseeable future, just as they increasingly have been for more than three decades.[24] Over the past twenty-five years, women have composed more than 50 percent of college graduates in this country and can be found in every field, even those that continue to be associated with men.[25] While some debate women's innate aptitude for math and science, the fact is that in 2006, 16.1 percent of degrees awarded to women and 15.7 percent of degrees awarded to men were in science and engineering.[26]

Today nearly 60 percent of all college graduates are women, a fact that prompted the dean of admissions and financial aid at Kenyon College to write a *New York Times* op-ed apologizing for the "demographic reality" that "because young men are rarer, they're more valued applicants."[27] Women are also outperforming men in college, graduating with better grades and more honors, and demonstrating leadership and contribution to their communities more often.[28] The number of women in college is also filling the pipeline of the educational ladder, so that women now represent over 50 percent of those receiving master's degrees. With respect to professional degrees, women now compose half of all law students, close to half of medical students, and over 40 percent of MBAs (see figure 2-6).

Women are not only filling the pipeline in colleges and graduate schools; they are also filling the pipeline at work. Women make up almost half the workforce, and their representation at work is growing at a faster rate than that of men. Women are projected to account for 51 percent of the increase in total labor force growth between 2004 and 2014.[29] They already account for 50 percent of all workers in management, professional careers, and related

FIGURE 2-6

Percentage of professional degrees awarded to women

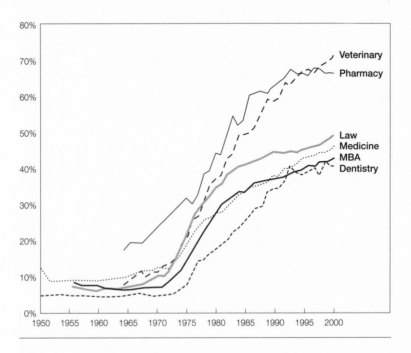

occupations. Women actually *outnumber* men in such occupations as:

- Financial managers

- Accountants and auditors

- Budget analysts

- Loan counselors and officers

- Human resource managers

- Education administrators

• Medical and health services managers

• Property, real estate, and community association managers[30]

Moreover, recent studies by Harvard Business School and Catalyst agree that companies with higher percentages of women in their executive ranks deliver comparatively higher levels of profitability and stock-price growth. These findings are similar to those of another study assessing the impact of women in large enterprises.[31] In a 2006 survey of the two hundred largest publicly traded companies in California, the University of California–Davis Graduate School of Management concluded that companies with women in top leadership positions have "stronger relationships with customers and shareholders and a more diverse and profitable business."[32] Yet despite the positive impact women are making across these and other key metrics in the corporate world, employers, particularly in industries such as information technology, continue to have a particularly hard time attracting women.[33]

Even though women are in the workforce to stay, the fact is that most women, particularly those with children, do not have the same career trajectories as men. A survey of over sixteen hundred men and women graduates of twelve top-ranked business schools revealed that, while 72 percent of white men with children have worked continuously full-time, only 22 percent of white women with children have done so.[34] Results of the Harvard Business School study, noted in chapter 1, of its own graduates from the classes of 1971 through 1981 are worth repeating here. While 89 percent of the men were working full-time five years or more after graduation (their prime career-building years), only 56 percent of the women were—and of the *women with more than one child, only 38 percent were working full-time.* The remaining 62 percent of women with more than one child were working part-time or not at all.[35]

For many women, the career paths within their organizations are colliding with their biological clocks. Because of the impact of children on women's career trajectories, it is important to understand the vast changes that have occurred since 1970 in terms of whether and when women marry and when they start having families. Many women now marry and have children later in life. As a result, 81 percent of households with children under eighteen are headed by parents who are between the ages of thirty-five and forty-four.[36]

Meanwhile, the ranks of married women in the workforce have nearly doubled since 1970 (see table 2-1). This combination of delayed child raising and active participation in work and careers has created a dilemma for many women. They are starting and raising families precisely when they are expected to accelerate their way up the corporate ladder and when top performers especially are expected to be gunning for leadership.

Off-Ramps and On-Ramps: Keeping Talented Women on the Road to Success, based on a survey of more than 2,400 women and

TABLE 2-1

Changes related to women, family, and work

	1970	2000
Percentage of women who had never been married by their early thirties*	6%	22%
Median age of women at first marriage**	21	25
Percentage of first births to women age 30 or over**	7%	22%
Percentage of married women who were in the workforce*	32%	62%

*Phyllis Moen and Patricia Roehling, *The Career Mystique: Cracks in the American Dream* (Lanham, MD: Rowman & Littlefield, 2005), 49.
**U.S. Census Bureau, "Maternity Leave and Employment Patterns of First-time Mothers, 1961–2000," *Current Population Reports* (Washington, DC: GPO, 2005).

653 men ages twenty-eight to fifty-five, confirms that women's lives do not fit with the current work structures the way men's lives do.[37] All the survey participants were categorized as "highly qualified"—with either a graduate degree, a professional degree, or a high-honors undergraduate degree. Of these, "fully two-thirds of highly qualified women have discontinuous or nonlinear careers."[38]

The survey also found that 37 percent of women and 43 percent of women with children took a voluntary leave at some point in their careers, compared with only 24 percent of men, regardless of their parental status.[39] While 44 percent of the women cited "family" reasons (including both child care and elder care) for taking a leave, only 12 percent of the men did. Instead, 29 percent of men left to "change careers," and 25 percent of men left to "earn a degree or other training."[40]

Although the media has portrayed women's decisions to opt out as a final one that contains an undercurrent of indictment against the workplace (as in women are "voting with their feet"), the reality is actually quite different. The vast majority of women who step out of the workforce want to return. In the "Off-Ramps and On-Ramps" survey, almost *all* (93 percent) of the women who left want to return to their careers.[41]

In a similar study conducted by the Wharton Center for Leadership and Change Management, 87 percent of the women surveyed said they intended to return when they left work.[42] It's interesting to note that women who did leave the workforce, for whatever reason, were away for an average of only 2.2 years.[43] And a Yale Women's Center survey indicates that only 4.1 percent of Yale women plan to *completely* stop working after they have children, and just under three-fourths say they'd take less than one year off after their children were born.

Nor should the movement of women in and out of the work-force be seen as a sign that they lack ambition: many women aspire to the corner office, even if they can't follow a straight path to get there.[44] Because women do not always keep fresh their knowledge and networks when they step out of the workforce, they have a harder time reconnecting. This is true for even highly accomplished women whose reentry résumés glow with outstanding credentials in higher education and professional achievement and perhaps even nonprofit management or government service. These women, like others, are uncertain of how they *can* reconnect and, for that reason, are also uncertain of how they *want* to reconnect. The fact is that they rarely are hired even by the corporations attracted by their previous experience and capabilities.

Most organizations are also ill equipped to make reentry possible, let alone easy. Take Citigroup, for example. Chairman and CEO Chuck Prince made work-life flexibility programs one of the global financial services giant's five strategic priorities in 2005. Management committee executives often suggest potential reentry candidates to each other for screening interviews. Yet so far, Citigroup has been unable to adapt its recruiting systems to identify and place reentry women into suitable available roles. "It's frustrating," says Hans Morris, chief financial officer, and head of finance, operations and technology for Citi Markets & Banking. "For women who want to get back in, there is no organized point of sale for them. They're not saying, 'Well, it's July and I've got to gear up for recruiting season' or 'I've got to prepare myself and do all these things because there is a predictable cycle that I understand.' So when we look at a résumé, we ask, 'What could this person do? What could I do with them?' She'll meet with six or seven people. At the end of the day, you often decide that you can't hire her because you are not certain. It's only 1 in 100 connections where you say, 'OK, we'll try you here and we'll see what happens.' It is very apparent to me that once you drop out temporarily, it is very hard to get back in."[45]

All of this makes the complete exit of women from the workforce—even for a short period—very costly to both the employer and the employee. Nevertheless, Citigroup sees an opportunity and is in the early stages of "trying to figure it all out," Morris added.

The vagaries of trying to make their lives fit into their work are not lost on women in the workforce. Younger women in particular are highly aware that the Pace, Workload, and Location/ Scheduling of work in their careers—and perhaps even their Roles— will have to change for various periods once they start families. But they are not sure which employers will allow these adjustments. We call this "anticipatory career anxiety." One recent twenty-eight-year-old graduate of Harvard Business School—we'll call her Amy—told us she rejected an attractive offer for a full-time position at a prestigious strategy consulting firm for just this reason.

Amy said she was worried that her biological clock would collide with the intensifying career demands she likely would encounter within a few years at the consulting firm. "I didn't want to put myself through that," she said. Few of the women partners at that firm had children, which she found "a little scary." She added that she didn't want to "face the choices that I think the women partners had to make." Instead, she accepted an offer with a consumer products company where she had worked one summer. Several women held senior positions in the company, and she was persuaded that the company "will be flexible for people who they think are good and want to keep." She added, "Women on [business school] campuses talk about these choices incessantly. It's a huge issue."

The bottom line is this: women are a major source of talent for the foreseeable future. However, there is a clear mismatch between how careers are structured and women's lives, especially the lives of women with children. Therefore, if companies are going to be able to grow—and get the most out of their talented women—they will need to create ways for women to contribute at work throughout the course of their lives.

TREND 4: CHANGING EXPECTATIONS OF MEN

When women first started asking for flexibility, men remained silent. Men were likely to view family and work as separate responsibilities. They used unspoken and informal means to make the two coexist. Women, however, from the beginning were more likely to consider family and work to be interdependent. It was natural, then, for women to pioneer the development of formal flexible-work programs.[46] Yet, as noted earlier in this chapter, men are spending more time with their children than in past decades, and many have reached a point where preserving or increasing their personal time is a growing priority.[47]

When *Fortune* magazine surveyed male executives whose average age was just over fifty and who worked on average fifty-eight hours a week, 64 percent said they would choose time over money, and 71 percent said they would choose time over advancement. Nearly half of them strongly agreed and another third somewhat agreed with this statement: "I would like job options that let me realize my professional aspirations while having more time for family, community, religious activities, friends, and hobbies" (see figure 2-7).[48]

In a large study of men and women senior executives, three-fourths of whom are two or fewer reporting levels from the CEO,

FIGURE 2-7

Male executives who want job options that let them have more personal time

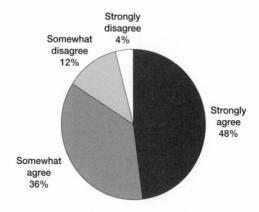

Source: Jody Miller, "Get a Life!" *Fortune,* November 28, 2005.

there was a surprising similarity between men and women in terms of what types of flexibility they would like to have available to them and use, although women were more likely to both want and use these options than men (see table 2-2). Men as well as women are currently placing high value on having control over their schedules. A 2006 study by the Association of Executive Search Consultants found that "more than half of senior executives polled would go so far as to turn down a promotion if it meant losing more control over their schedule."[49]

Moreover, these sentiments only become stronger in surveys of workers of younger-generation men who, as we discuss in the following section, place higher priority on family and life outside work. The convergence of changing roles for men and changing expectations of younger generations is evident in the fact that young men are more directly involved in child care and other family

TABLE 2-2

Use of FWAs

Women	Currently use	Would like to use	Have used in the past
Compressed workweek	3%	28%	7%
Telecommute/work from home	13	23	12
Reduced work schedule	1	17	8
Flexible arrival/departure time	44	9	8
Leaves/sabbaticals	1	39	7
Change work schedule ad hoc	20	14	4
Change work location ad hoc	9	13	3

Men	Currently use	Would like to use	Have used in the past
Compressed workweek	2%	24%	5%
Telecommute/work from home	12	15	14
Reduced work schedule	1	14	1
Flexible arrival/departure time	36	6	11
Leaves/sabbaticals	1	32	2
Change work schedule ad hoc	18	9	6
Change work location ad hoc	9	11	5

Source: Catalyst, *Women and Men in U.S. Corporate Leadership: Same Workplace, Different Realities* (New York: Catalyst, 2004).

responsibilities than older men.[50] According to Families and Work Institute, Gen X fathers spend significantly more time with and caring for their children than boomer fathers with children of the same ages—an average of 3.4 hours per workday versus an average of 2.2 hours for boomer fathers.[51]

In fact, research conducted by Catalyst suggests that men feel as much or more work-life conflict than women.[52] "It's hard to say why men are reporting such high levels of work-life conflict," said

Ellen Galinsky, president of Families and Work Institute. "It may be that men are newer at the multitasking reality that women have lived in for a long time, or it may be that men feel less permission to do something about it."[53]

Some men are taking dramatic action to achieve their desired career-life fit. Twelve percent of men leave their jobs every year to have more family time.[54] That being said, most men are just wishing they could take advantage of flexible options. Thirteen percent of men currently working full-time schedules would prefer to be working part-time. Nearly half of men, 49 percent, would prefer to have part-year work schedules.[55] Men are also as likely as women to want to be able to work some hours from home.[56]

Men's latent demand for flexibility in the workplace may be higher than reported because, historically, flex options were dressed in maternity clothing. In an article in the *Ivey Business Journal,* Professors Kerry Daly and Linda Hawkins explain how traditional gender notions create a formidable environment for men to ask for flexibility: "For men, a number of forces in the workplace make it difficult to speak up for flexibility. It is manifest in the expectation that men take leaves only when they really have to (why isn't your partner doing this?), that men are at greater risk of compromising loyalty when they choose family over work, or that men use parental leaves as a way of increasing their leisure time. With these residues of traditional gender expectations actively playing out, we can understand why the workplace is not an environment that encourages men to confidently take advantage of any workplace strategies offered."[57]

A look at the number of men who take advantage of paternity leave programs is one obvious indicator of how deep seated this lack of permission perceived by men really is. Overall, only 5–15 percent of men eligible for paternity leave actually take advantage of it.[58] Many men will not take paternity leave because they worry they will be viewed as less committed to their work.[59]

So, as employers move forward to create new paths for women to contribute at work in a variety of ways throughout the course of their lives, employers should recognize at the outset that these new systems also must factor in changing career-life attitudes of men and, as you'll see in the following section, the next generations.

TREND 5: EMERGING EXPECTATIONS OF GENERATIONS X AND Y

Nowhere is the convergence of men's and women's desires and expectations regarding work more evident than in Generations X and Y, who make up the majority of the workforce in many knowledge-based companies. Members of this "family-first generation" place a priority on having a meaningful family life and are less willing to make the sacrifices regarding family life that so many boomers made.[60] In a study of professionals in their mid-twenties to midthirties, Catalyst found that 84 percent of respondents said that "having a loving family" was important, while only 21 percent said that earning "a great deal of money" was important. Men and women differed in their emphasis on these and other factors, but they did not differ on how they ranked such factors (see figure 2-8).[61]

Similarly, Families and Work Institute found that boomers were almost twice as likely to be work-centric (defined as "putting your job before your family"), compared with only 13 percent of Generations X and Y (see table 2-3). The remaining 87 percent of Gen X and Y are either family-centric ("putting family before work") or dual-centric ("placing the same priority on family and work").[62] Even when the study controlled for children at

FIGURE 2-8

Importance of work-related and personal and family values by gender

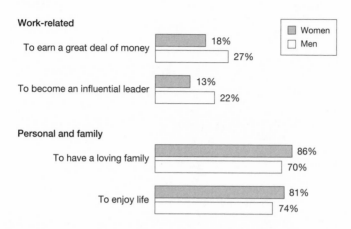

Source: Catalyst, *The Next Generation: Today's Professionals, Tomorrow's Leaders* (New York: Catalyst, 2001).

home under the age of eighteen, Gen X is more likely to be family-centric than boomers. (Most of Gen Y is too young to have children at home.)

Generations X and Y have high expectations for both their personal lives and their work lives. While their parents may have emphasized financial success, the younger generations value personally challenging and interesting work over compensation.[63] "Both men and women of these generations are working hard and hesitate to climb the corporate ladder because they don't see how it allows them to maintain their dual-centric values," says Galinsky of Families and Work Institute.[64]

Generations X and Y also seem interested in creating unique paths that allow them to pursue and achieve all their life goals. We

TABLE 2-3

Work priorities across the generations

Relative priority placed on work versus family	Gen Y (under 23) N = 250	Gen X (23–37) N = 855	Boomer (38–57) N = 404	Mature (58 or older) N = 276
Work-centric	13%	13%	22%	12%
Dual-centric	37	35	37	54
Family-centric	50	52	41	34

Source: Families and Work Institute, Generation & Gender in the Workplace (New York: American Business Collaboration, 2004).

believe this lofty vision will hold for countless Gen X and Y members as the new "true north" on their compass of generational convictions. Gen X and Y have already made a significant impact on workplace culture. They are curious and collaborative but at the same time can be impatient and demanding.[65] Gen X and Y expect frequent constructive feedback from their managers and open, upward communication channels.[66] The younger generations are technologically savvy and adaptable to change; they are willing and often seek ways to work with nontraditional methods and schedules.[67]

It is not possible to say for certain whether new career-life attitudes cited in Gen X and Y studies will persist in whole or in part throughout the course of these generations' careers. Yet directional shifts underpinning these new attitudes are undeniable and unlikely to change. Gen X and Y have an optimistic and ambitious idea of what they want and can achieve in their careers. They envision a career as a personalized path that meets an individual's interests and development goals and includes many diverse work experiences.[68] Our research has found that they don't necessarily see this as being disloyal—rather they view loyalty as a two-way street where they are willing to give and grow in exchange for being given the opportunity to do so.

However, "more than twice as many people between the ages of 14 and 21 would prefer job mobility *within a single company* [emphasis added] as would choose career advancement in the open market," concluded a 2004 joint study by Deloitte and the Institute for the Future.[69] But, if these younger workers can't find this mobility within their companies, they are prepared to move around. Without the notion of lifetime employment or the corporate promise of pensions, as in the past, there isn't anything to hold them back.

TREND 6: INCREASING IMPACT OF TECHNOLOGY

If silicon is the crude oil of the information age, then broadband, laptops, mobile phones, PDAs, and an expanding array of other digital devices are the cars, ferries, and airplanes of the always-on communications era that the silicon chip has made possible.[70] As software progressively links these technologies—directly, and collectively, to the Internet and other powerful networks—organizations continually have new tools to change long-standing rules about where, when, and how work gets done. Technology is paving the way for employers—and employees—to offer creative virtual workplace options.

A major driver of virtual offices has been the explosive growth in broadband connectivity. In 2000, less than 5 percent of U.S. households had broadband connectivity, but by October 2006 the number had risen to over 76 percent.[71] Other digital technologies that support remote work have growth stories similar to that of broadband: e-mail is ubiquitous, instant messaging and text messaging are pervasive (especially for younger generations), and cellular phones have become commonplace, growing from 92,000 in 1984 to more than 150 million in the United States today.[72] Worldwide cellular phone penetration rates are even higher.

Virtual private networks have enabled home users to gain secure access to corporate applications. These private networks often are used by a company or by several companies to transmit confidential information over a publicly accessible network, such as the Internet. Then, too, the advent of thin-client (server-based applications puts both applications and data on the network rather than on individual computer hard drives. This gives knowledge workers access to their electronic desktops from any nearby client—without the tether of their laptops, where their applications and data files were previously resident. Videoconferencing, too, has grown, albeit more slowly than many predicted in the post-9/11 environment.

Collectively, these technologies make it possible to think about work processes in exciting new ways. Indeed, business leaders and other organizational architects have new opportunities to apply "an inventive mindset to not just technologies, but to organizations," says Thomas W. Malone, management professor at the MIT Sloan School of Management.[73] We've entered a world in which it is not uncommon to find the call center agent, the executive headhunter, and/or the entire IT department working virtually, traveling to various corporate locations as needed and working from their homes or another location the rest of the time. Take JetBlue Airways or 1-800-Flowers, for example, whose customer service representatives work comfortably from their home offices or kitchen tables.

Another twist on the technology-enabled workplace is the way high-performing specialists increasingly control more terms of employment. Shelly Lazarus, chairman and CEO of Ogilvy & Mather Worldwide, one of the world's largest marketing communications firms, recalls how a freelance creative director named David living on a ranch an hour from Dallas, Texas, set down one nonnegotiable condition for his full-time employment: "He said, 'I'll work for you, but I'll only do it from my ranch.'" Lazarus says she knew he was serious when he added, "There are 26 planes a day that go between Dallas and New York, so if you need me, I can be there." The lesson? Advancing technology not only opens the aperture for how and where work gets done; it also gives high performers more bargaining leverage. "When there's only one David, you have to have him on his terms," says Lazarus.

While this may be a far-reaching case (no pun intended), many other examples of virtual workplaces are now becoming possible thanks to enabling technologies. The natural tendency in the early years of any significant technological advancement is to extend current practices into the future. For example, the first cars looked like carriages; early television programs were basically radio shows with pictures; early Web sites looked a lot like books; and so on. So, with history as our weather vane, and as technology continues to advance, new models of how, where, and when work gets done will continue to open up new workplace possibilities.

Sun Microsystems' core business is creating innovative technologies to accelerate workplace innovation and productivity. Sun has made innovation a priority within its own $13 billion global organization. Take the recent collaboration of its real estate, information technology, and human resource organizations. These units of the Silicon Valley–based company built an infrastructure to support employee telecommuting, "hoteling" in temporary offices at Sun properties, and virtual teaming.[74] Talent management goals were embedded in the project's business objectives. They included reducing operating costs, leveraging the network to the greatest possible extent, finding talent nationally and internationally, entering emerging markets, engaging more extensively with global customers, and ensuring business continuity when the unexpected happened.

In 2006, more than 50 percent of Sun's thirty-four thousand employees were active participants in this program, known as Open Work™. Employee participants worked in Sun offices only part-time or, if designated for home-based assignment, not at all.[75] The cost savings in the five years between 2001 and 2006 were more than $387 million. On top of these substantial bottom-line benefits, the company also was honored for enabling employees to choose more creatively where and when to work when the non-profit Alliance for Work-Life Progress gave Sun one of three 2006 awards for Work-Life Innovative Excellence. The Open Work program has also been recognized for its benefits to the environment and Sun's commitment to eco-responsibility—helping to reduce carbon cmissions from employees by taking them off the road.

A paper Sun published on its Open Work program noted that "[t]oday's markets are increasingly distributed, and even for smaller enterprises, the competitive landscape is increasingly global. New digital technologies are providing the emerging workforce with unprecedented choices in where to live and for whom to work. Indeed, the 'knowledge workforce' expects to have such choices made available to them."[76]

In addition to where and how the work gets done, technology is enabling another workplace movement. "Technology is also instigating a profound change on how employees are measured," says Robyn Denholm, senior vice president of corporate strategy planning for Sun. "Face time, for example, is no longer a criterion in employee performance—it's measured by the output or the value that is being contributed."[77]

"It is about driving competitive advantage," Denholm continues. "We are a global technology company whose core strategy is rooted in product innovation. Our people are the creators of that innovation. Creating the Open Work environment was a way for us to further enhance the quality of life for our people—and also enabled us to save significant money in the process." It turns out that the Open Work program also helps the environment, avoiding an estimated thirty thousand tons of carbon dioxide emissions each year.[78]

While these workforce trends we've traversed are driving significant employee requirements for flexibility, varieties of new technologies are enabling unprecedented possibilities for designing how and where work gets done. Information-age technologies are creating marvelous opportunities for employers and employees, and as we've seen time and again, technology also has a way of accelerating change.

Each of these six trends is well under way. In fact, we are now at the *end of the beginning*—the beginning of an era set apart ever so gradually from the mid-twentieth-century labor pool that preceded it by what has become a workforce far more diverse and varied in its profile. For the next ten to twenty years, three different generations unusually divergent in their attitudes, beliefs, and expectations will coexist in the same workforce and in the same organizations.

Meanwhile, the convergence of these six key trends is already in play, forcing a reshaping of workplace policies and systems. The availability of skilled knowledge workers is falling. The evanescent profile and values of the traditional family structure have been replaced by multiple new variations. The percentage of women in the skilled labor segment is expanding, with the absolute numbers of women likely to soon exceed absolute numbers of men in most knowledge-driven organizations. The percentage of men committed to the job-first/family-second ethos of the boomer generation is declining. Moreover, the new career-life attitudes of Generations X and Y suggest both increased wariness of today's high-pressure workplace demands *and* increased desire for many diverse work experiences.

For all these reasons, the *new* traditional workforce is becoming more diverse than ever in terms of its background, personal circumstances, expectations, and aspirations. Many executives believe that their organizations already are far down this road, embracing flextime, telecommuting, leaves of absence, and other common elements of flexible work arrangements. But as we explain in the next chapter, despite the applause from the many workers who benefit, these arrangements are not adequately helping companies increase loyalty and long-term relationships with their most qualified and vital employees. In short, flexible work arrangements are simply not the solution we all hoped they would be.

THREE

Why Flexible Work Arrangements Are Not the Answer

What I dream of is an art of balance.

—Henri Matisse

When it comes to our lives and our careers, more of us are thinking like Matisse. We envision lives that artfully balance a passion for work and for personal interests, and more of us are trying to find ways to pursue these dreams. Formal flexible work arrangements have been a first step in our attempts. They provide options other than the traditional workplace expectation that employees will work continuously and full-time and do so consistently in the office. But by focusing on relatively short-term personal situations while ignoring longer-term career implications, FWAs mainly have served as way stations in career paths, sidelining—and even derailing—the careers of FWA program participants.

Major companies have had FWA policies since the 1990s, and some have had them for more than twenty-five years. We refer here to the formal FWA policies and programs that allow employees to work outside an organization's normal requirements and career paths (see table 3-1). Organizations have also responded with informal flexibility, enabling employees to leave work early to coach the soccer team or arrive a few hours late to accommodate a doctor's appointment, or in other ways provide occasional adjustments in work schedule and sometimes even work location.

Informal flexibility does foster a more open environment and more give around the workplace edges and has been used by many

TABLE 3-1

Typical FWA options

Flextime	Have flexibility with arrival, departure, and/or lunch times in conjunction with defined "core times" of the workday, during which employees are required to be present (nonflexible hours)
Reduced hours/part-time	Switch between full-time and part-time work schedules for periods and receive prorated compensation
Compressed workweek	Arrange work schedule to complete total weekly work hours in fewer days than the regular workweek
Telework/telecommuting	Work some hours from home
Job sharing	Share job responsibilities among multiple employees
Banking of hours	Aggregate hours worked over an extended period (annually or semiannually) to achieve total hours for that period so that employee has flexibility over when he or she works
Gradual retirement	Reduce workload or number of work hours during period before retirement
Leaves/sabbaticals	Arrange extended periods off from work without compensation

employees, particularly women, as a way to help manage their day-to-day responsibilities.[1] However, both informal flexibility and formal FWAs suffer from the same flaw: both are point-in-time responses and not a systemic solution to the structural issue of how to align the workplace with the evolving workforce.

Many business leaders and managers presume that their FWA programs and policies *do* provide adequate options for greater career-life fit and deliver a payback of increased employee satisfaction and lower turnover. This presumption is often not realized in practice, however. The purpose of this chapter is to describe the many reasons for these failed expectations.

Despite a workforce that is clamoring for more flexibility, there is mounting evidence that FWAs are not the answer for retaining top performers and developing long-term relationships between employers and employees. There is one overarching reason for this: FWAs are point solutions often expressed as one-off accommodations or exceptions; neither are they adequately integrated with the organization's ongoing talent management processes, nor do they address the larger question of how an individual's career unfolds over time. In short, FWAs lack connection with the construct of careers.

THE CAREER CONTINUUM

One consequence of using FWAs as point solutions is that they are interpreted as static. This is in part because employers and employees typically view the job—rather than the career—as the unit of measure. As a result, life needs are not viewed as a continuum but rather as a static set of circumstances that must be balanced against current work needs.

Work-life balance became part of common business language in the 1980s as women entered the corporate workforce in unprecedented numbers and corporations responded with these new programs. In our view, though, *work-life balance* is an unfortunate phrase because it denotes a sense of opposing forces—work versus life—and a steady state betwen them. We argue that work and life are intertwined and, therefore, must always be considered in tandem (see figure 3-1). (Note our use of the term *career-life fit* to represent this symbiotic relationship.)

Once work is recognized within an organization's policies and practices as a part of a career and, ultimately, the cycle of life, then workforce structures will be set in the context of the myriad ways in which lives across the different generations in the workforce unfold. This recognition includes both the microlevel of determining how work gets done and the macrolevel of determining how

FIGURE 3-1

Transition from "work-life balance" to "work as a part of life"

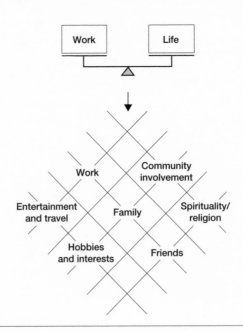

careers are built. Workplace sociologist Phyllis Moen and fellow scholar Stephen Sweet make this point powerfully in their landmark Ecology of Careers study. The study, based on interviews conducted with more than forty-six hundred people between 1998 and 2002, provided a window into how modern-day employees cope with workplace turbulence produced by "American policies and cultural myths out of step with 21st-century realities."[2] In a subsequent article, Moen and Sweet described what we now regard as part of the underpinning philosophy for a corporate-lattice organization: "A life course perspective on the topic of 'work and family' moves the discourse away from one of individuals, and their conflicting or enabling role obligations at any one point in time, to a focus on dynamic relationships between roles and among individuals as lives unfold: (1) over time, (2) in tandem, and (3) in particular contexts . . . This involves reframing and broadening the 'work-family' issue to one of 'careers' as they unfold in multi-layered contexts and over the life course."[3]

We recognize that this is much easier said than done, especially when the main tool available has been FWAs. Employees and their supervisors confront but rarely resolve the many pragmatic hurdles that appear when creating and managing FWAs. The trade-offs are oblique, at best, and often go unspoken. Mismatched expectations are common on both sides of the aisle.

DOING THE SAME THINGS WHILE EXPECTING A DIFFERENT RESULT

FWAs have not achieved their promise across corporate structures. One example is in the accounting profession, where studies by the American Institute of Certified Public Accountants found that FWAs do not sufficiently improve the retention of employees struggling to balance their career and life demands. The majority of public accounting firms have been aggressive in implementing FWA policies over the years, yet the two most prevalent reasons why employees leave are still (1) working conditions (schedule, hours, assignments), cited by 90 percent of the women and 80 percent of the men, and (2) work-life issues, cited by 86 percent of the women and 70 percent of the men.[4]

Many *Fortune* 500 companies have also implemented FWA policies to help retain talented women, yet the turnover rate for women in corporations continues to be higher than for men.[5] While women have long cited lack of flexibility as a major reason for leaving, men are increasingly concerned about this issue as well. In a 2006 study of employees in medium and large companies across industries, when those who had recently joined their organizations were asked what were the key factors in their decision, men were more likely than women to cite work-life issues as a top factor.[6] If FWA policies were having the desired impact, then why is the very issue they are meant to address still a top reason for turnover?

Utilization rates are another key indicator that FWA policies are not meeting the needs of employees. Even though 96 percent of law firms offer FWAs, only 4 percent of all lawyers actually take advantage of these programs at any time.[7] Is it possible that 96 percent of lawyers don't have any interest or need for FWAs? No. In fact, more than a quarter of women and one-fifth of men in law firms are interested in reduced work schedules.[8] In addition, more than half the men and women in the legal profession would take advantage of some type of nonstandard working relationship, at least occasionally, if they didn't consider it such a risky proposition. Yet most lawyers do not take advantage of FWA policies because they believe those who do are viewed as uncommitted— or are even blacklisted—and, therefore, limited in career prospects.[9]

This stigma or "career penalty" attached to FWAs has been widely documented. Families and Work Institute, a respected think tank on workplace and workforce issues, has found that close to 40 percent of working parents—the very group that FWA policies target—believe their jobs would be in jeopardy if they worked flexibly.[10]

Similarly, a majority of senior executives said they did not use FWAs because of the anticipated negative career consequences. Only 15 percent of women and 20 percent of men thought they could use an FWA without impairing their career progress. Additionally, a mere 24 percent of women and 33 percent of men thought they could turn down a promotion for family or personal reasons without a career penalty.[11] Clearly, any deviation from the norm of working continuously full-time is risky in the eyes of those who have made it to the top of the corporate ladder.[12]

So what's going on when there is apparent alignment between the increasing need for greater workplace flexibility and the well-intentioned FWA benefits offered by many organizations, yet the results just aren't there? The answer is rooted in the fact that most FWAs do not address the structural conflict between the corporate ladder's rigid approach to building careers and the fluid needs of employees to create career paths that reflect the changing priorities in their lives.

In fact, FWAs are positioned as compromises to the ideal of full-time employees who traditionally would do anything to climb the corporate ladder. Viewed in this way, FWAs actually reinforce the traditional structure of the linear, continuous career path because they are not perceived as realistic options for serious, career-minded employees. FWAs are not seen as a way to get to the top.

On the contrary, they are widely perceived as a signal of an employee's lack of ambition to climb the corporate ladder. In their book *The Career Mystique: Cracks in the American Dream*, Phyllis Moen and Patricia Roehling came to the same conclusion. They wrote: "People will take advantage of flexible work-hour and career options only if they are not one-way exits from real jobs, but are viewed as legitimate time-outs or alternative pathways."[13] It stands to reason that as long as flexibility is addressed only at the margin through FWAs, it can deliver only marginal results.

THE MEN WON'T EVEN GO THERE

Let's take another look at why FWAs are not the answer to the evolving workforce. While women have been willing to pay a price in their career potential in exchange for more flexibility, men thus far have not. To be sure, as noted in chapter 2, men of all ages hold changing views about a salaried life committed to climbing the corporate ladder.

In a 2006 survey of salaried employees in medium and large corporations, 31 percent of men said work-life balance was a primary source of dissatisfaction.[14] So FWAs would seem a reasonable option for many—in the form of compressed workweeks, part-time schedules, job sharing, and so on. But men overwhelmingly reject FWAs as being for women only, a kiss of death for their careers, regardless of how accomplished or indispensable they are in the eyes of peers and superiors.[15] "There is a perception that FWAs are for women who don't want to work full-time and are looking for a way to cut back to three days a week," says one senior executive at a large professional services firm who spoke to us. "I would bet there is not a single male in our group who is on an FWA."

The recent career shift of a rising star senior manager, we'll call him Rafael, illustrates the problem men in particular have with FWAs. You might have considered Rafael an ideal FWA candidate. He enjoyed and excelled at the client work he pursued for nine years in the corporate world following ten years as a navy pilot, earning an MBA degree along the way. Yet, working long hours while his wife raised their three children at home, Rafael increasingly was gripped by a serious family concern. A hormonal imbalance had led to unpredictable behavior swings for his oldest son, now a teenager. Rafael concluded that as a responsible father he must spend more time with his son, be available immediately if any crisis occurred, and move his family from the Midwest closer to the West Coast home of his aging parents.

The solution he and his supervisors created was a new, internally focused, full-time role: developing innovative services and client offerings that others would take to market—instead of working directly with often unpredictable schedules with his long-time external clients. Interestingly, an FWA was never even discussed as an option for Rafael. His supervisor said switching to an FWA would have knocked him out of consideration for promotion. And, he said, an FWA was not appropriate because Rafael wanted to continue in a full-time role. The lesson? In the eyes of many senior-level executives and rank-and-file employees in even the most progressive workplaces, FWAs appear irretrievably consigned to the equivalency of male career suicide.

Put bluntly, employers believe the FWA crowd can't be counted on. This is especially true if the FWA is in response to the professional's caregiving responsibilities. As described in the National Academy of Sciences report *Beyond Bias and Barriers*, working mothers and fathers—whose caregiving responsibilities at home are well known at work—often face subtle, unconscious bias regarding their competence and commitment. According to the report, "[M]others experience gender stereotyping in how jobs are defined, in the standards to which they are held, and in assumptions that are made about them and their work; for example, a man who is absent is assumed to be presenting a paper, whereas a woman who is absent is assumed to be taking care of her children . . . Similarly, fathers who take parental leave or even a short leave to deal with family matters often receive fewer rewards and lower performance ratings and are viewed as less committed."[16]

With more men, particularly those in Generations X and Y, looking for corporate-lattice options in a corporate-ladder world, we expect few will embrace FWAs as a realistic choice when they examine how to dial down on the Pace, Workload, or other dimensions of their careers. In the corporate-ladder world, you are moving up the ladder—or moving off. (Practically speaking, there is little opportunity to move down the ladder.) Rather than experimenting with FWAs, we predict more men will decide to step off just as women have historically done.

In fact, it's already happening. Generation X men in their late twenties and early thirties who "see the chutes in the world as interesting as the ladders," as the *New York Times* puts it, are willing to quit jobs, taking weeks or even months off to achieve their version of career-life fit before reentering the workforce.[17] Jesse Keller, then a thirty-two-year-old software engineer, left his employer after ten years in 2006 to visit all fifty-eight national parks. "As the retirement age pushes farther back and the finances for that time of life are less and less certain, it was almost unconscionable to not take advantage of the opportunity to travel now when I had the money and the health," he told the *New York Times.* Keller said he was more worried about encountering another burnout work experience in a new job than searching for that new job after his parks tour ended. "The trick is finding a job that has the balance built in so that I don't have to go off on a grand adventure to recover from work," he said.[18]

Changing jobs is a normal and frequent part of work life for Generations X and Y. A Families and Work Institute study of Generation Y employees found that they were 18 percent more likely to quit their jobs than baby boomer employees when those boomers were the same age as the Gen Y employees in the sample.[19] FWAs are no match for the increasing complexity of the workforce in terms of what Gen Y employees want out of work and what they are willing to trade off to get it.

To be sure, FWAs have worked—and do work—well for some people. Today, most FWAs still are used by women, primarily working mothers whose motivations are usually shaped by child care and schooling issues. Many individuals (mainly women) who have taken advantage of FWAs say that they would have left their employers if not for this option.[20]

Despite pockets of success, though, very few organizations have been able to scale their FWA programs into a companywide retention strategy. For instance, when an $8 billion professional services organization conducted thirteen focus groups over three months in late 2005, 50 percent of participants said their FWAs were working well for them. But the remaining 50 percent stated categorically that their FWAs were *not* working for them. This split down the middle suggests how difficult it is for organizations to achieve consistent standards on quality and effectiveness in FWA programs.

STRAIGHT TALK ABOUT FWAS: WHAT MANY SEEM TO KNOW BUT NO ONE SAYS

In the spirit of promoting candid discussion about FWAs, we offer the following synopsis of their pitfalls and limitations.

FWA Programs Don't Scale

Even a well-designed FWA program typically is implemented on an ad hoc basis and negotiated case by case.[21] There are two main problems with an ad hoc approach: it is very difficult to manage for both real and perceived parity in the eyes of employees, and it is nearly impossible to scale. Citigroup, for example, has had a flexible work policy for years, but "I would describe it as an ad hoc policy," says Hans Morris, a member of Citigroup's management committee and a leader in its markets and banking units. He adds: "We are just beginning to really approach this in a systematic way. There are certain things that have been instituted, but if you compare those policies and plans to the whole year-end compensation plan, for example, one is extremely highly developed, and the other is in the early, early stages of trying to figure it all out. We recognize that this is something we need to do. We want to allow for less linear, more radial paths in career progression."[22]

The Reason for an FWA Matters (Even Though It Shouldn't)

From a legal standpoint, while FWAs cannot be available to mothers without also being available to fathers, the reality is that many managers are much more willing to discuss and approve an FWA with a woman who is struggling with young children than a man who wants to scale back because his wife also works outside the home. Although the reason shouldn't matter, many managers routinely make isolated judgments about which reasons are more "important" than others.

The Higher You Go, the Harder It Gets

When FWAs do work, they seem to work best for people who are individual contributors rather than managers and leaders. But individual contributors eventually move into leadership or management roles. Making an FWA work at the more senior levels is harder, and some companies just won't do it. Gap Inc., for one, a retailer with a hundred fifty thousand employees and $16 billion in revenues, revised its FWA policy to explicitly require senior executives to work full-time.[23] This is not unusual, although making it public may be. Many companies will not consider employees on reduced-hour FWAs for advancement to senior positions. This creates the proverbial "mommy track"—or dead end—that makes FWAs unappealing to ambitious, talented employees.

The FWA Candidate Doesn't Always Fit the Job

One common response by managers presented with an FWA request is to move the individual into a job that at least appears to fit—such as moving a researcher into an administrative role or moving a salesperson to a desk job. However, if these moves are driven simply by the employee's need for flexibility without regard to his or her strengths, skills, and training, the employee may not succeed in the role. When this occurs, the work arrangement—rather than the mismatch of talent with the job—often gets the blame in the eyes of managers, team members, and other employees.

Managers Are Between a Rock and a Hard Place

In many companies allocating budgets for employee head count, benefits, and other fixed costs assumes full-time status. Adjustments for part-time workers, job-sharing arrangements, or those who work from home on a part- or full-time basis are difficult to make. This issue can be particularly acute for FWA employees who retain health and related company benefits. The costs per hour of FWA employees can be significantly higher than those for full-time colleagues, which can skew departmental allocations for general and administrative expenses. Along with the hard costs, FWA employees can disproportionately consume more of supervisors' time. Past experience wrestling with this tangible and intangible overhead can turn managers against approving or even considering FWAs. Conversely, managers who put time and energy into managing FWAs well often are not recognized for it. They don't get credit for avoiding turnover or juggling internal and external resources to achieve performance targets. Misaligned incentives cause some well-intentioned managers to stay away from FWAs.

Managers Fear Entitlement Status

Even though FWAs are not the same as benefits, when a manager allows a high performer to go on an FWA, weaker performers may insist that they are entitled to the same deal—because it is only "fair." Anticipating this, some managers may either resist giving an FWA to anyone on their team or simply negotiate with the high performer on a one-off basis, cutting a deal that works for the individual but is outside the system. These one-off deals, however, come with their own set of issues. One is potential resentment among coworkers, especially if terms of the one-off deal are not visible to them. Another is coordination, especially if these one-off deals proliferate as more and more team members negotiate for them. And while we're talking about managers, we should also mention that some are simply dead-set against approving FWAs for one simple reason: it's just not the way *they* climbed the ladder.

Adjusting Performance Expectations—and Ratings— Is Complicated

Many intangibles go into an employee's performance evaluation. Even when evaluation metrics for reduced-schedule FWAs are recalibrated against those for full-time employees (which doesn't always happen), how do you judge the "extracurricular" efforts of reduced-schedule employees against those of full-time employees who regularly contribute through mentoring, recruiting, office activities, and involvement in community affairs? How much of these activities should be expected of someone on a reduced schedule? What if the employee doesn't choose to put in those extra hours, precisely because he or she is on an FWA?

And while we're talking about hours, in cutting-edge knowledge organizations in particular, there's a big difference between an employer's agreement of three days a week and an employee's interpretation of twenty-four hours a week. Consider the case of Anna, a manager who typically worked fifty-plus hours, just like her peers. She requested and was granted a reduced schedule, working three days a week. To her it meant twenty-four *hours* per week (three eight-hour days), but to her employer, the expectation was three ten-hour days—a five-day, fifty-hour week reduced proportionately by 40 percent. Without consistent guidelines for supervisors, grading these "soft" factors is tricky. Then, too, if the evaluation system requires forced rankings, how do you justify giving someone who has worked long hours and sacrificed a great deal personally the same or even a lower rating than the person working a part-time schedule, no matter how well he or she has performed? The answer is that it rarely happens.

No One Wants to Talk About the Trade-offs

With FWAs expectations are usually not managed well and misunderstandings are commonplace. Why? Because people don't want to talk about the trade-offs. The most obvious trade-off, reduced compensation in line with reduced hours and contributions, is often addressed, but many others are not. For example, issues regarding the range of potential assignments open to someone working from home two or three days a week, or how a reduced schedule can impact promotion opportunities, frequently are either unresolved or overlooked. This may happen because

FWAs are pieced together at a crisis point, when an employee is close to leaving the organization. The employee and supervisor are more focused on the short-term fix. Neither typically has much experience with FWAs, so the broader, long-term career implications rarely are part of their conversation.

Someone Has to Pick Up the Slack

Another pitfall that can easily derail an FWA is the question of who picks up the slack for those who work a reduced schedule. Employees working in the office each day can feel that they are the only ones asked to stay late when a deadline is looming. FWAs exacerbate this problem. James J. Sandman, former managing partner of the law firm Arnold & Porter, says, "The person who doesn't have a family can conclude that a family obligation is a professionally acceptable reason for not being available for late-night or weekend work. On the other hand, friends visiting from out of town are not considered an acceptable reason to say no."[24]

FWAs Can Create Feelings of Inadequacy

The flip side of these situations for many professionals on FWAs can be feelings of inadequacy. Trying to be significantly involved at home and contribute at a high level at work can leave the employee feeling that he or she isn't doing *anything* well. It's dispiriting for FWA employees because they often feel they are working two jobs—one at home and one at work—but their efforts are not recognized in either sphere. Their lives are a complicated web of schedules, commitments, and deadlines that often pull them in many directions. Such employees may feel they are constantly swimming upstream, reminding people repeatedly of their schedule. When your team decides to hold its team meetings on Wednesday, you remind everyone Wednesday is your day off and then await (silently, usually) their sighs of burden and annoyance. These day-in, day-out reminders of being out of sync with coworkers can wear down even the most persistent and ambitious employees.

Commitment Is Questioned

There is another source of mistrust or confusion: when the commitment of people on an FWA is questioned. FWA employees often are perceived as being less committed to both organization and career than someone in a traditional full-time role. As noted earlier, the perception and reality of a stigma or career penalty attached to FWAs has been widely documented.[25] What results is a vicious cycle: if you are on an FWA, the prevailing view of managers and peers is that you must not be as committed as someone working full-time. If you are viewed as less committed to the organization, managers will not invest in you in the same way they invest in a full-time employee. If you view the organization as less committed to you, it is more likely you will disengage over time and, indeed, become less committed to the organization. This downward spiral is discouraging for FWA employees as well as for employers. FWA employees often feel that their teams and managers are simply waiting for the ball to drop, as opposed to appreciating current efforts as indications of commitment and resolve. Meanwhile, supervisors often believe that the considerable time and effort they invest to make FWAs work are not recognized by their FWA employees. They perceive these employees as being more caught up in protecting their FWA than in contributing to the team's success. And many supervisors are convinced that few FWA participants ever return to a traditional full-time career path.

These straight-talk points represent in the best of circumstances a complex balancing act among supervisors and employees—a balancing act that occasionally evolves into successful long-term contributions and rewards for both parties. More likely, these points collectively describe a series of failures and disappointments that waste the scarce resources of the organization and the talents and aspirations of the employee. In the worst case, of course, some don't even get the option of a one-off deal.

THE CASE OF SHEILAH—OR SOMEONE YOU KNOW WHO SOUNDS JUST LIKE HER

Sheilah Eisel was a top sales performer at a global software company the day she told her supervisor she was pregnant. No problem. The company was eager to keep her active in the business, and she agreed to return part-time, three days a week, after her maternity leave. "I thought, 'this is perfect,' and it actually worked out incredibly well—for about three months," she said in a 2005 segment on the CBS News program *60 Minutes.*[26] Although Sheilah was on a three-day-a-week schedule, in practice the company didn't adjust her workload or change her sales role. What was intended by both sides as an FWA failed.

Before long Sheilah was logging forty hours "on a slow week" and often as many as fifty or sixty hours, she said. Moreover, the sought-after client accounts she once managed were being handled by other colleagues. "How am I going to give you the top accounts?" Sheilah recalled her manager saying, over her protests. "You're only here three days a week."

The answer, she said, was changing her workload to just one account. It was true, Sheilah acknowledged later, that she could not handle several top accounts working part-time and keeping baby play dates. "But if I had one top account," it could have worked, she says. Yet no one in a position to make the decision thought to change either her role or her workload to fit her part-time schedule—or to craft a new schedule to match a new work agenda. Sheilah's typical workweek exceeded fifty hours despite her part-time arrangement. Like so many others, Sheilah ultimately quit.

It doesn't have to be this way. With the quest to find and retain talent increasing in intensity, companies that understand the connection between the structural inadequacies of FWAs, the rise of nontraditional family structures and their inherent conflict with the traditional workplace, the attitudes of the younger generations, the changing attitudes of men, and the increasing importance of women to achieve business objectives begin to solve the problem.

In the same *60 Minutes* news program in which Sheilah described her failed FWA experience, Kim B. Clark, then dean of Harvard Business School, said businessmen who had invested in talented women "for years" often told him that their failure to retain these women was driving them "crazy." The businessmen's problem, Clark said, was that "they're asking the wrong question. The right question is: 'How do we "change" to keep this talent active and involved with us?'" We couldn't agree more. We would simply add that this "wrong question" syndrome applies also in corporations' misreading of changing attitudes about the waning imperatives of corporate-ladder careers among both men and women.

The bottom line is this: FWAs aren't the answer because they don't address many of the day-to-day or longer-term realities and requirements of a person's career. They are not the answer because they are often stand-alone, ad hoc responses with little or no linkage to the organization's talent management systems that clarify roles and responsibilities, training and development tracks, performance evaluation criteria, benefits, compensation, succession planning, and related programs.

FWAs are not the answer because they do not factor in the individual's longer-term employment trajectory—career steps, further development, the next career stages, and so on. They are not the answer because they have not achieved the desired impact in increased employee satisfaction and loyalty. Ultimately, FWAs aren't the answer because they don't work for the employee—and, therefore, don't work for the employer (and vice versa).

A structural and attitudinal shift from the ladder to the lattice is in the offing. Within the next few years, FWAs increasingly will be viewed as an interim late-twentieth-century workplace solution, a transitional step that helped individuals cope with new work and personal demands amid historic changes in U.S. society and the U.S. workforce. FWAs are not the answer to the talent shortage corporations are confronting, nor are they the options employees require to create long-term careers in these corporations.

Henri Matisse was one of the great artists of the twentieth century. Matisse trained first as a young artist with rigid styles of painting before turning to "much freer and more expressive" styles and ultimately a new medium of simple collages.[27] We believe an analogous transformation is afoot as organizations work to rebalance the scales of the traditional workplace and the nontraditional workforce. MCC provides managers and employees an alternative system that interprets the employee's life and work as a fluid set of mutually reinforcing needs that must be taken into account together, over time. In the next chapter, we describe how this transformation can be achieved and some signs that it is already under way.

FOUR

Mass Career Customization

The Framework for Aligning
the Workplace with the Workforce

If you put people in a world class environment,
they will give a world class performance.

—Bill Strickland

Building a corporate-lattice organization requires first and foremost a new mental model. As noted in chapter 1, lattices are prized by mathematicians as uniquely elegant structures that can be repeated at any scale in the theoretical world. In the real world, lattices are platforms for growth, with upward momentum visible along their varying paths. This is precisely the new kind of organizational model that knowledge workers are seeking to advance their careers in tandem with their changing personal lives.

Building a latticelike organization also requires a rock-solid business case. Outlined in chapter 2, our case rests first on the irrefutable evidence of a shrinking pool of skilled labor, rising ratios of women to men in knowledge-driven organizations, and changing family structures. Combining with these forces is the reality that younger generations, in conjunction with boomer men, are less motivated by the possibilities—and more cognizant of the life trade-offs—of what they view as a winner-take-all corporate-ladder lottery. These converging social forces underscore emerging realities for employers about the varied career paces and patterns of their workers.

This new normal characterizes today's nontraditional work-force, which is both complex and multifaceted. It presents an urgent workplace challenge, a quantum leap from the conventional ladder culture that most twenty-first-century business leaders accepted when their careers got off the ground.

It is also why this new latticelike mental model—along with the supporting framework, approach, and processes—is urgently needed to identify, develop, and advance talent in ways that go well beyond the one-off marginal systems of flexible work arrangements. MCC is that framework. (See figure 4-1 for why we use the term *mass career customization.*)

This chapter describes MCC in detail—its core characteristics, principles, and elements. A corollary discussion on how to begin implementing MCC is presented in chapters 5 and 6. Through these three chapters, we offer a guide and even some cautionary notes to help you organize, standardize, and, yes, even scale a cooperative approach to career development and planning that allows individuals to customize career paths over time. It's a lofty goal, but one whose time has surely come.

FIGURE 4-1

Why call it "Mass Career Customization"?

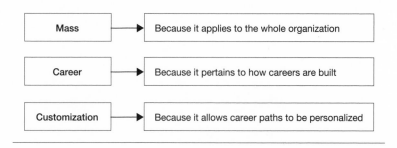

MCC supports a customized approach to career development that engages the individual as a partner in his or her development—and signals the organization's commitment to each individual's growth. And it creates a connection with the employee much in the same way that mass product customization increases customer loyalty.

MASS CUSTOMIZATION IS ALL AROUND

We are increasingly familiar with products in our daily lives that enable us to customize various features to our tastes and wants. For instance, you can track package shipments through the customized online pages of your favorite postal carrier, monitor price changes in your investment portfolio, follow news of specific topics of choice at the *Wall Street Journal*'s My Online Journal, and even order from among two hundred thousand possible combinations of colored M&M candies at www.mymms.com (see the box "My M&M's: 200,000 Consumer Choices Via Mass Product Customization").

My M&M's: 200,000 Consumer Choices
Via Mass Product Customization

Since 2004, any customer can go to the My M&M's online shopping service and devise (in theory, at least) as many as two hundred thousand different order combinations from among candy pieces produced in twenty-one colors, including light blue, dark pink, and aqua green, among many others. This is an everyday example of mass customization and quite a change from the first twenty years of the confection's history, when Forrest Mars Sr. sold the candies to consumers in any color they wanted—as long as it was the same dark brown color he first shipped to U.S. soldiers during World War II. And the proof is in the pudding: sales of M&M's from online customization products have doubled every year since 2005, with more than two thousand orders placed *each day*.[a]

Mass product customization is becoming pervasive. Think of something as common as U.S. postage stamps—now you can add your favorite photo to postage. Other examples include designing your

MIT professor Frank Piller, a thought leader in mass customization, found three areas of economic benefit in his 2004 study— "Does Mass Customization Pay?"—that are associated with mass product customization: the customer's willingness to pay more for customized products, supply-chain cost savings, and increased customer loyalty.[1]

We believe these benefits are readily transferable to MCC. Our thinking is if consumers and producers see the advantages of customers' being more actively involved in product design by next pair of athletic shoes—choosing the colors, sole design, and size—or configuring a personal computer that is specifically assembled to your order. Whenever you join in any of these shopping habits, you are spinning the wheel of mass product customization. Mass product customization has benefited both consumers, by giving them more choices, and producers, by increasing customer satisfaction and generating greater customer loyalty while strengthening the brand along the way.

Rapidly advancing technologies of low-cost communications, Internet-based connectivity, and computer-aided design and manufacturing capabilities brought early adopters of mass product customization onto the scene in the 1990s. Fast-forward to today when the results are important—and competitive—new product sets that integrate these technologies with consumer research, marketing communications, product innovation, and sales.

a. Kristi Ledford, e-mail to Jenna Carl, November 7, 2006.

customizing the buying experience, why not apply these same basic concepts to the relationship between the employer and the employee?

Mass career customization moves organizations away from the one-size-fits-all view of career progression toward supporting multiple career paths, each designed and executed through continual collaboration between employee and employer. (To be sure, the organization sets the options boundaries.) The important recognition here is that MCC provides the structure for better collaboration between employees and their managers and offers a sustainable, scaleable solution to realign today's outmoded workplace with the evolving modern workforce.

THE CORE CHARACTERISTICS OF MCC

MCC is centered on the view that, increasingly, the career journey of many employees in the knowledge-driven organizations of the twenty-first century will look similar to a sine wave of sorts, with climbing and falling phases. Corporate-ladder organizations, even those with model flexible work programs, can neither accommodate nor scale these varying career-life phases. The customized, undulating path requires an ongoing collaboration between the organization as a whole, the manager, and the employee, each of whom subscribes to a culture that embraces career options—options that fit the needs of the business and the needs of the individual today and over time.

"With an MCC approach, corporations are not saying, I want only your good years or the years in which you can make a maximum contribution," says Harvard's Professor Myra M. Hart. According to her, corporations are instead saying to employees, "We really want a lifetime contract with you. We know that some years you will be giving more and some years you will be giving less. But that's fine as long as we can plot this in a way that works and makes sense for both of us." She added, "This is a very new approach to employee retention."[2]

MCC assumes a definite, not infinite, set of options along four career dimensions and provides a structure to articulate and manage these options as commonplace events—rather than one-off accommodations. Employees customize their careers by selecting the option within each of these four dimensions that most closely matches their career objectives while considering their life circumstances and the needs of the business at any point in time. Decisions on each option are made in counsel with managers and revisited periodically. These choices are registered on an MCC profile, as illustrated in figure 4-2.

Figure 4-2 is a visual representation of one point in the career of a sales manager. It is labeled "common," meaning that his profile looks similar to 90-plus percent of employee profiles at any given point in time. Let's examine briefly the node settings in each of the four dimensions in relation to his current situation. The setting in the Pace dimension is near the center of the continuum, indicating he is on a midrange track toward promotion, with increasing authority and responsibility. He is working full-time with no restrictions, meaning he travels whenever necessary and without any limit on work location. (In other words, Workload is recorded at the "full" level, and Location/Schedule is set at "not restricted.") The setting for Role, several nodes down the continuum, signals he is a midlevel manager.

The MCC profile provides a snapshot of this sales manager's career at a given point in time, *and* it can be adjusted over time. We like to compare it with setting and adjusting the sound equalizer on a home entertainment system, where you move sliders up or down the vertical slots (bass, midrange, treble, etc.) to set the desired level of sound. The slots define the range of dimensions—the degrees of richness of the sound. A visual display of lights outlines the loudness (or softness) of sounds. Moving the sliders adjusts the output to get the optimal mix.

Just as you would move the sliders up or down to set the level of sound, MCC allows employees to dial up and down along the four

FIGURE 4-2

"Common" MCC employee profile

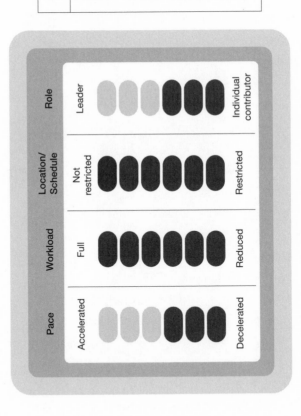

	Pace	Workload	Location/Schedule	Role
	Accelerated	Full	Not restricted	Leader
	Decelerated	Reduced	Restricted	Individual contributor

The four dimensions of MCC

Pace
Options relating to the rate of career progression

Workload
Choices relating to the quantity of work output

Location/Schedule
Options for when and where work is performed

Role
Choices in position and responsibilities

dimensions to optimize their career paths at varying life stages. Just as with the sound equalizer, the goal of MCC is to calibrate the settings to deliver the desired mix at any given time. Figure 1-3 in chapter 1 introduced the idea of how these settings can change over time. Different settings adjustments at each of Tina's five profile stages reflect the modest changes in Pace, Workload, Location/Schedule, and Role along her career progression. Viewed together, Tina's career dimensions ebb and flow over her five distinct career phases.

Before further examining the four career dimensions and the interplay among them in more detail, let's step back for a moment to underscore the core characteristics that distinguish MCC as a career management process:

- *MCC is fluid.* It eliminates the more linear and binary, up-or-out, on-or-off characteristics of the corporate ladder and replaces them with an adaptive framework. By its very nature, MCC encourages adaptability and longer-view thinking as core competencies of both manager and employee. This, in turn, creates a more transparent workplace with multiple career-path options. The ability to discuss and assess how work is getting done, and to make adjustments that directly address the changing needs of the individual and the business, become part of the way the organization itself works. In a world that is characterized by accelerating rates of change, expertise in managing change well is a goal of many leading organizations.[3] Regular conversations and transparency around multiple career-path options are ways in which MCC is fluid and promotes better alignment between talent management processes and business objectives.

- *MCC is multidimensional.* First, it identifies and acknowledges the four core career dimensions—Pace, Workload,

Location/Schedule, and Role. These four dimensions are inter-dependent and should always be viewed in this way, not in isolation. Second, MCC adds the perspective of a career moving through time, acknowledging that needs and priorities change over an individual's work life.

As a new centerpiece of the career management process, MCC makes it more natural for supervisors and employees to discuss how employees' needs and priorities are expected to change throughout the course of their career.[4] In turn, it should be easier for supervisors to identify, understand, and respond effectively to the myriad career and workplace priorities that exist across the different generations now in the workforce.

- *MCC is applicable to everyone.* In this way it creates the "new normal" for shaping career paths within lattice organizations. This is a key distinction between MCC and FWAs, which are applied as accommodations only to those who request, and are granted, exceptions to the long-standing one-size-fits-all standard of full-time regular employment. While organizations may develop eligibility thresholds for the MCC framework, everyone who meets them will be part of MCC. Over time, this structure becomes part of the lexicon in performance review, compensation, goal-setting, and similar conversations that routinely take place today.

- *MCC offers transparency.* Since every employee has a four-dimensional profile that outlines where each is relative to Pace, Workload, Location/Schedule, and Role, MCC promotes a transparency that, by its very nature, encourages fresh thinking by each team member and his or her manager regarding potential career paths. Transparency of chosen career options among various team members also reduces team dynamic issues that often surface when members perceive disparities or preferential treatment.

In this way, MCC transforms the idea of fairness from a static assumption—that each employee should, except for FWA accommodations, conform to the traditional full-time standard—to a more dynamic notion of fairness relative to each employee's profile. "There's a larger notion of fairness in the MCC approach," says Ogilvy & Mather's Shelly Lazarus. "The fairness is allowing people enough freedom to work in the way that fits their needs, that fits their lives. So it's a more abstract notion of fairness than work hours or location or anything like that."[5]

These core characteristics of MCC address the limited effectiveness and root issues of FWAs examined in detail in chapter 3: the stigma associated with exception-based arrangements and the point-solution orientation of FWAs. (See figure 4-3 for a comparison of more differences between MCC and FWAs.) MCC adapts

FIGURE 4-3

Comparison of FWAs and MCC

Flexible work arrangements	Mass career customization
• Exception based	• Mainstream and foundational
• Point solution	• Fluid and dynamic over time
• Limited in scope to where and how much work gets done	• Includes longer-term career considerations as well as how and where work gets done
• Generally perceived as career limiting	• Career enabling
• Often not engaged in the culture	• Engrained in the culture
• One-off; difficult to scale	• Scalable
• Reactive	• Proactive
	• Transparent

over time using the employee's career path, rather than the present job situation, as the unit of measure. MCC also creates a set of variable paths and, in doing so, replaces outmoded assumptions and biases of corporate-ladder organizations that continuous full-time employment over an entire career is not only expected but, indeed, likely the only way to progress.

Breaks or interruptions along this track in ladder organizations are viewed as exceptions—and, as noted in the previous chapter, often are perceived by managers as a signal of the employee's lack of long-term commitment. Replacing the career-ladder norm with a career lattice over time will reduce and ultimately eliminate the stigma that in most organizations is still associated with deviations.

OPTION VALUE IS GREATER THAN OPTIONS TAKEN

So does this mean that in any given organization, there will be as many different profiles as there are people? On the contrary, we found that at any point in time the vast majority of individuals—more than 90 percent—have profiles that look just like the standard profile in figure 4-2.

If this is so, then why evolve into a lattice-type organization? In part because of its *option value.* Studies show that giving employees decision-making power and options in managing their career results in greater job satisfaction.[6] Employees care more about having control over their flexibility options than they do about having any one particular option available to them.[7] Employees who believe they have some level of control, or options, in setting priorities and organizational support are happier, more loyal, and more productive.[8] "Our people know that if they needed to do something differently that we could probably work it out," says Lazarus. "That's a very important message for me to send to everybody."

Employees receive a psychic benefit in knowing that, even though there may not be a need to deviate from standard full-time employment today, options are available should the need arise sometime down the road. Many workers, both men and women, take comfort in knowing that there is an organizational process in place to dial down (or up, as the case may be) if and when needed. Ruby, once a high-performing, high-potential manager in a services company, is typical of many employees who left an employer because that option value did not exist. "I really liked my job and the company I was working for, but I couldn't see a way that it could work now that I have a child," she says. "I wound up leaving so I could get settled and build a track record within a different industry and employer where things would be much more predictable."[9]

From the employee's perspective, option value is an enduring, important benefit of MCC. The absence of options was a key issue in Amy's employment decision, as we described in chapter 2. The recent Harvard Business School graduate rejected an offer from a prestigious firm, concluding that her anticipated desire to modify intensifying career demands when she was ready to start a family would be unwelcome. Women, in particular, are looking ahead, many beginning in their early twenties, trying to anticipate *if* and *how* they can achieve their dreams for both career and personal ambitions. If they can't see a way within your organization, they will go in a different direction. Men are increasingly doing this as well.

There is a cultural value, of sorts, that MCC delivers as well. MCC requires well-framed conversations between employee and employer to examine trade-offs associated with choices along the interdependent dimensions of the framework. MCC makes these choices more visible and more explicit. In these conversations both manager and employee are responsible for discussing the options and trade-offs associated with varying paths of dialing up, dialing down, or simply staying the current course. Both also are responsible for revisiting these choices along the way as part of normal career-planning or goal-setting cycles, since career decisions often are set—either explicitly or implicitly—during these discussions.

The transparency and shared responsibility for career planning that result from these structured conversations are integral features of a corporate-lattice organization. A better partnership between an employer and employee in designing and building careers over time will be more satisfying to both sides. Individuals will feel more confident about their choices because they are making them with more complete information and an understanding of the range of options available to them. Managers will have a clearer, more candid picture of what their employees are able to contribute. This will help them better align the work with their resource planning and avoid unexpected leaves of absence or resignations—especially of their higher-potential staff, who have more external as well as internal options. In fact, by engaging the employee in designing his or her career, MCC builds loyalty that will mitigate against these allures.

ELEMENTS OF THE MCC FRAMEWORK

Now we're ready for a closer look at the four dimensions of careers: Pace, Workload, Location/Schedule, and Role. We define career dimensions of MCC in generic terms that a majority of organizations can readily relate to. We invite you, however, to tailor these terms and the endpoints on the continuums based on the particulars of your organization's business model, structure, culture, talent management stresses, and the like. This is an important point. Not all MCC systems will look exactly the same—although each will reflect the evolution from a ladder to a lattice model.

Every eligible employee will have an MCC profile, though most of these profiles are essentially the same in depicting the norm: full-time, fully-engaged, and nonrestricted careers. While we wholly expect the vast majority of employees will have very similar profiles at any given time, it is likely that *employees will not all have the same standard profile continuously over time.*

To underscore a point made earlier in this chapter, as you read through the description of each MCC dimension that follows, keep in mind that collectively the dimensions are interdependent; that is, dialing up or down in one dimension can require adjustments in one or more of the other three dimensions.

Pace

The first dimension, Pace, addresses how quickly an employee is slated to progress to increasing levels of responsibility and authority. The progression typically is signaled by formal promotion from one level to the next. There often are an anticipated number of years associated with each move upward. For example, within brand management, the track is often two years as an assistant/associate brand manager, then one to two years as a brand manager, followed by two or three years as a senior brand manager.

The two endpoints are "accelerated" and "decelerated" with varying grades in between. These are relative terms that reflect an organization's judgment about what competencies, experiences, tenure, and attributes are needed at each level. Pace is the dimension that most clearly incorporates the element of time. This is because Pace relates to a sequence of work contributions and rewards that evolve over months and years rather than through day-to-day work activities.

The tenure track is a classic example of a clearly defined Pace dimension that has been modified by educational institutions seeking to respond to the fact that some faculty cannot work continuously full-time throughout the tenure-track years. Princeton University is one of several leading universities that have instituted automatic extensions of the tenure track for both men and women when they have children. Another example is MIT, which automatically extends the tenure clock for women faculty who bear a child. Similarly, UC Berkeley requires that evaluators of candidates for positions ignore any time extensions on candidates' CVs due to family responsibilities.[10]

Law firms have also modified the partner track to allow those who are not working continuously full-time to advance, albeit at a slower pace. For example, Vinson & Elkins extends the time span available for promotion to partner for associates working less than a full workload, based on the percentage of full-time work they do.

Workload

The Workload dimension addresses the quantity of work performed, typically measured in units of hours or days per week, pay cycle, or month. We use "full" and "reduced" as the endpoints on the Workload continuum. These terms correlate directly with the full-time and part-time vernacular used today in most organizations. Workload can be tied to performance measures. For example, if a full-time exempt employee is expected to work fifty hours a week and seeks an 80 percent Schedule, this would equate to forty hours a week. Or, if a sales manager working full-time is expected to generate $5 million in sales, then the workload of a sales manager working a 60 percent Workload would be targeted at generating $3 million in sales.

It is important to consider in Workload calculations the expected contributions to activities not directly tied to an employee's job performance. These may include time spent recruiting, mentoring, and organizing office events.

Companies are experimenting with everything from project-based work to disaggregating jobs into modules of work tasks. The Business Opportunities for Leadership Diversity project, a Sloan Foundation–backed effort to help CEOs create competitive advantage in the global economy through workplace innovation, has been testing team-based work redesign in several companies, including the Chubb Group, Pitney Bowes Inc., Johnson & Johnson, PepsiCo, and Puget Sound Energy. Selected teams in each company designed their work schedules and workloads to achieve their business performance goals while also meeting the personal needs of team members. Results have been promising, with productivity and morale rising significantly.[11]

Location/Schedule

Where work gets done (Location) and *when* work gets done (Schedule) are combined in this career dimension. Together, Location and Schedule define much of the day-to-day experience of *how* work gets done. The actual range of movement or change possible is segmented at points along a continuum between "restricted" and "not restricted." Restrictions can take the form of working remotely, compressed workweeks, off-cycle hours (such as noon to 8 p.m., rather than 9 a.m. to 5 p.m.), and so forth.

Face-time cultures—which either implicitly or explicitly require employees to be physically present in the office for a set period of time on a regular basis—dominate the traditional approach to Location/Schedule. While technology advances have created many more choices along this dimension, changing attitudes about providing more latitude over where and when work gets done are also important.

Consider Best Buy's Results-Oriented Work Environment (ROWE) experiment. Participating workers can work "when and where they like, as long as they get the job done."[12] Employees create their own schedules providing they demonstrate ability to complete their work via the arrangement. Employees may work different hours on different days; they may work from home, the office, or perhaps somewhere else if they'd like.

Begun in 2002 with three hundred employees, by 2005 ROWE had grown to include thirty-five hundred employees. It is still experimental. Departments figure out how to manage themselves, with many creating different systems for staying connected and getting work done despite the lack of uniform schedules and locations among the staff members. The program's growth and popularity are testaments to both the demand for this type of work arrangement and its potential success. Operating results also are positive, with productivity in participating departments rising smartly and average voluntary turnover plummeting.[13]

Role

For most companies, the Role dimension is likely the one that will be tailored the most based on the nature of each organization's business. Role refers to the category of an employee's position, job description, and responsibilities. In a variety of organizations, industries, and professions, Role (as reflected in the MCC framework) can range from an individual contributor performing specific tasks, even at a high or sophisticated level (think of a scientist working on a research project), to a manager or higher level positions engaged in leading others, supervising relationships, and overseeing work activities and output.

For global companies, Role may have the added dimension of international assignments. In a services organization, Role may be viewed along the continuum of activity between external client-facing positions (which is, on average, 80 percent of the business) and internal staff-oriented positions (like marketing, finance, HR, and IT). For demonstration purposes, we define the endpoints of the Role continuum as "individual contributor" and "leader."

American Express has experimented with the Role dimension in a pilot study at its OPEN business unit, allowing employees to shift from their current role to serving as an internal consultant working on specific projects.[14] The American Express pilot study has developed tools and processes to analyze talent supply (consulting resources) and talent demand (project work) along with a system to match the two. (For a synopsis of each MCC dimension, see table 4-1.)

Now let's consider how the four dimensions are very much interdependent. For example, a schedule of three days per week would impact Location/Schedule but would also likely affect Workload (if it is not a compressed workweek arrangement). This, in turn, may impact Pace to the degree that the Workload adjustment would limit the experiences or skills necessary to progress to the next level. Similarly, a management role may well require being available at certain times (impacting Schedule) more than the role of an individual contributor who may not be required to be as accessible to others up, down, and laterally throughout the organization.

TABLE 4-1

Summary of MCC dimensions

Dimension	Description	Scope	Points on continuum
Pace	Options relating to the rate of career progression	• Expectations for time in role and time to promotion • Expectations for reasonable and likely progression path	• Accelerated to decelerated
Workload	Choices relating to the quantity of work output	• Number of assignments • Types of assignments • Adjunct activities—recruiting, office morale activities, involvement in community programs, etc.	• Full to reduced
Location/ Schedule	Options for when and where work is performed	• Ability to travel • In-office or remote work location • Specific hours in day(s) per week (or other time interval)	• Not restricted to restricted • At home or at the office
Role	Choices in position and responsibilities	• Position • Responsibilities • Work assignments • Span of management	• Line versus staff • Individual contributor to leader

For a vivid example, recall Sheilah Eisel's *60 Minutes* story in chapter 3. When Sheilah cut back to three days a week from five, her manager failed to adjust her workload proportionately with her reduced schedule but did take her off key client accounts, thereby changing her role. Without the framework of MCC, neither Sheilah nor her manager had the tools to properly adjust her career path to her life circumstances, which ultimately resulted in her resignation. Table 4-2 provides examples of how the four dimensions relate to each other.

TABLE 4-2

How MCC dimensions impact each other

As driver	Pace	Workload	Location/Schedule	Role
Pace		Desire for accelerated pace is likely not possible with a reduced workload	Desire for accelerated pace may reduce options for restricting location/schedule	Desire for decelerated pace may eliminate options for positions that entail significant management responsibilities
Workload	Desire for a reduced workload may decelerate pace		Desire for a reduced workload may or may not be linked to location restrictions, such as working from home	Desire for a reduced workload may result in an individual contributor role
Location/Schedule	Desire for a reduced schedule may slow pace, but desire to work from home on limited basis may not affect pace	Desire for a reduced schedule will likely result in reduced workload		Desire for location/schedule restrictions may eliminate possibility of a role that requires travel or in-office presence
Role	Desire for specific kind of role may determine pace of career progression—and destination of career	Desire for specific role may increase or decrease the options for modifying workload	Desire for specific role may reduce the options for location/schedule restrictions	

NOT AN ISLAND

The four dimensions and their interplay are the core of the MCC framework, but the framework is not static—nor is it meant to operate in isolation. Rather, it is meant to function within an organization's overarching talent management systems and processes. MCC provides a useful, unifying lexicon that can and should traverse across a complement of talent management processes, including:

- Roles and responsibilities

- Scheduling and deployment

- Goal setting

- Career planning

- Professional training and development

- Succession planning

- Performance evaluation

- Compensation and benefits

Organizational adoption and mutual reinforcement are the two primary reasons for embedding or in other ways connecting the MCC framework to your existing talent management systems and cycles. Additional reasons are to:

- Provide immediate scale capability

- Bring career planning to the forefront, making it an intentional rather than a haphazard discussion

- Facilitate tracking of MCC's impact on talent management

- Provide managers and employees with guardrails that define options boundaries and shared business objectives

- Create a lexicon for one-on-one conversations between manager and employee and for informal discussions within teams and departments and across the organization

- Encourage greater transparency regarding career decisions across teams and between the employer and employee

We recognize that adding the MCC framework to goal-setting processes and subsequent cyclical talent management processes is not a simple matter. Our experience, however, is that using the MCC framework during goal-setting and performance review sessions sets a standard protocol, makes for a more robust discussion, and improves the efficacy of talent management processes. (We describe our experience with several MCC pilot programs in the next chapter.) For example, performance evaluations relative to goals, viewed through the lens of MCC, are more robust because the four dimensions have been calibrated to the individual's profile as well as to the organization's expectations for that person's contributions and growth.

In our view career planning does not happen consistently today. There is a widespread lack of organizational discipline and talent management rigor for career planning, as well as a lack of foresight within and across business units about the possibilities and the payoffs. For example, many managers assume that the best route for an individual to get to a certain place is to take the path that *they* took. Most organizations do not provide effective motivation for revisiting that simplistic assumption.

Another reason is that conversations about an employee's career ambitions and individual life needs are fundamentally personal.

Employees struggle with whether or how explicitly to share these details and where to draw the line. For their part, managers often are uncertain about legal constraints that apply in these discussions. We recognize that requiring the MCC profile conversation can raise predictably delicate issues for employees and managers, especially if their workplace relationship is new or the level of mutual trust is in doubt.

However, this is precisely why it is important to locate these conversations within existing, well-established systems. If you are used to manager-employee meetings and you use the MCC framework and lexicon as a matter of course, when the time comes for a dial-down request related to a personal issue, such as a new child or sick parent, it is less of a foreign concept for both the employee and the manager. Familiarity with these exchanges, even if previous ones simply confirmed a traditional path for the next increment of time, goes a long way in opening up communication. In fact, a significant benefit noted in early studies is that MCC provides a structure for conversations that until now lacked any guidance or boundaries and, as a result, have been shortchanged along the way.

It is important that each qualifying employee in the organizational unit is provided an initial MCC profile that reflects the four dimensions of his or her current work situation. As discussed earlier, this profile should then be included in subsequent discussions about goal setting, performance evaluation, career planning, and the like. By "qualifying employee," we mean that some organizations may choose to set some type of entry hurdle for eligibility into an MCC-type structure or program. One possible entry criterion is a minimum tenure level—one or two years, for example— so the employee has time to learn the organization, build both formal and informal networks, and so on. In turn, a minimum-tenure criterion gives managers more opportunity to get to know the employee and observe his or her performance in a variety of situations.

Another possible criterion is a minimum performance rating, such as "meets expectations" on a 5-point scale ranging from "significantly exceeds expectations" to "does not meet expectations." Some may set the entry hurdle at "meets expectations"; others may set it at "exceeds expectations" or better. Of course, neither of these sample criteria is mutually exclusive, and some organizations may choose to apply both tenure and performance eligibility hurdles.

To be sure, entry criteria are not a necessary component of an MCC program. However, there are varying points of view on this topic that you may want to consider. For some companies, participation in an MCC system, at least in the initial years of its implementation, is viewed as an additional benefit for higher performers that recognizes their contributions while providing an incentive for others. The opposing point of view, of course, is that resentment can build among team members who are ineligible for MCC under this system, and such ill will can undermine the program.

Our own view on this point has evolved as we've gained more real-life experience with MCC. Initially we held the view that it may be desirable to have tenure-based and perhaps even performance-based entry criteria for the reasons cited earlier. We now qualify our opinion on this point to include a word of practical caution: it may be more difficult to manage multiple systems (who's in MCC and who's not) than the benefits entry criteria may deliver.

When the MCC framework is fully operational, everyone in the organization (or all those who meet the threshold criteria, if any such criteria apply) will have an MCC profile. As described earlier, each MCC profile provides a snapshot of the employee's customized career path across the four dimensions for the current period. Over time, the dimensions and endpoints may evolve as each organization gains experience calibrating the endpoints to its structure, work patterns, and demands. Similarly, all the systems and processes that are linked to MCC will evolve as well, creating greater adaptability and elasticity within your talent management system—just what's called for by today's knowledge workers.

HOW MCC PROFILES WILL CHANGE OVER TIME

To appreciate the added value and pragmatism of the MCC framework over time—for both employee and employer—let's look at the career progression and shifting personal life priorities of an employee over nearly thirty years. MCC is new, of course, and an actual thirty-year example won't be available anytime soon. So we've crafted a composite story based on everyday workplace events and personal stories of a composite employee we'll call Gary. MCC profiles typically will be revisited yearly or even less often, though occasionally more frequently when unexpected events in an employee's workplace or life circumstances warrant. In our example we focus mainly on five career stages and in each case note the changes in some, or all, of the four MCC career dimensions.

As you can see in figure 4-4, ongoing adjustments in the nodes of each of the five MCC profiles create the sine wave effect described earlier. This dial-up/dial-down pattern over time, reflected in Gary's changing profiles, enables employees and their supervisors to actively pursue the right balance at any point and over the full course of an employee's work life.

Gary, an unmarried, twenty-seven-year-old MBA graduate, is hired by a global consumer products company into a fast-track

FIGURE 4-4

Gary's MCC profile stages

Career Years 0—3
Post-MBA/prefamily

Career Years 4—11
Young children

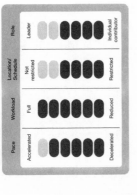

Career Years 12—20
Midcareer

Career Years 21—26
Teenage children

Career Years 27+
College-age children

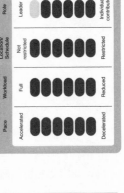

program combining brand management and marketing. The U.S.-headquartered company has more than thirty major product lines with total sales of $12 billion, markets in seventy-five countries, and thirty-five thousand employees worldwide, including twenty-five thousand in North America.

Gary's first assignment is assistant brand manager. He travels approximately fifteen days per month learning the business, participating in marketing campaigns, consumer research activities, and product research and development. He is promoted to associate brand manager after one year, a month after he gets married to a fellow MBA he met in grad school. The following year he is named brand manager for a popular line of soccer uniforms and related equipment, with responsibility for $50 million in sales and a team of twelve direct reports. His MCC profile shows that he is on an accelerated Pace with full Workload and no restrictions on Location/Schedule and that he is in a manager Role.

After Gary's first child is born, when he is thirty-one, he takes a three-month leave of absence after his wife's three-month maternity leave, returning to his brand manager position. He continues to work full-time but restricts his travel to ten days a month. Three years later, after his second child is born, Gary takes another three-month leave, this time after his wife completes a six-month maternity leave. He returns, working four days a week leading several product lines and contributing to both market research and corporate strategy efforts. This newly crafted, bimodal position enables him to focus more time and energy on his family. He limits travel to five to seven nights per month, stays current with rapid changes in the business, deepens his skills, and contributes his proven expertise as a brand manager, mentoring others along the way. Now thirty-seven, his Pace for promotion has slowed, but he and his manager agree that he will be in a strong position to shift back to an executive track when his youngest child enters kindergarten. His profile is adjusted to show a middle Pace, somewhat reduced Workload and restricted Location/Schedule, and a Role midway between individual contributor and leader.

Two years later, at the age of thirty-nine, Gary is promoted to vice president and overseeing three product lines; he has dialed up to five-day weeks and is working fifty hours a week and traveling an average of ten nights per month. His promotion Pace is again accelerated, and in another four years, Gary advances to group vice president, responsible for six product lines and more than $500 million in annual sales. His MCC profile shows accelerated Pace, full Workload, moderately restricted Location/Schedule, and leader-oriented Role. At age forty-seven, with his children now sixteen and thirteen, Gary decides to reduce his workload, travel, and schedule to be more involved with the lives of his teenage children. His brand portfolio is pared to four product lines, with $350 million in sales, and he takes on the lead role in an internal project. His profile is again adjusted to show a middle Pace, a somewhat restricted Workload and Location/Schedule, and a Role midway between individual contributor and leader.

In another five years, with both children in college, Gary is as enthusiastic and ambitious as ever about his work. He dials up again, expanding his executive portfolio to eight product lines and working full weeks with unrestricted travel and schedule. At age fifty-five, he is promoted again, to senior vice president, responsible for $1 billion in annual sales. His profile reflects this by showing a dialed-up Pace, Workload, Location/Schedule, and Role.

THE BENEFITS OF MCC

When employer and employee meet their responsibilities in the MCC framework, the potential positive outcome for the organization and the employee is tremendous. On a basic level, MCC provides real options for the employee to more effectively manage his or her life path and for the employer to more effectively manage its workforce. On another level, when well implemented, MCC has the ability to transform the quality of the relationship between companies and their employees, as we'll show in the next chapter, which results in far-reaching benefits for both parties.

The power of MCC is that it is framed, from the start, as an ongoing conversation between employers and their employees. In effect, MCC provides both parties a set of stepping-stones to place as needed across a stream of possibilities. These stepping-stones can lead to careers that collectively build a successful, market-leading talent pool.

For employers, MCC is a tool for attracting and retaining valued employees and for garnering greater employee productivity—reason enough to warrant its adoption. But over time the way that MCC can transform the relationship between employer and employee, and the way it can allow companies to accurately forecast their human capital resources, will have a significant impact. Greater understanding of employees' strengths and weaknesses, needs and aspirations, and life plans will give employers the ability to structure and manage their companies to greater potential. This will improve the employer's ability to accurately forecast talent needs, reducing costs, improving succession planning, and more efficiently targeting growth opportunities. Moreover, it will create greater job satisfaction and employee loyalty—which are sure to be in shorter supply as the labor markets continue to tighten.

As we've shown in this chapter, many companies have learned in the past few years that personalizing the *customer* experience is good for business. This effective marketing strategy—mass product customization—exploits new communications and manufacturing technologies to increase profit margins and customer satisfaction, build loyalty, and strengthen long-term brand affinity. Why not apply these same basic concepts to the workforce and the workplace?

MCC provides the framework, principles, and practices to increase employee engagement, satisfaction, loyalty, and long-term career aspirations with your organization. The MCC approach communicates a new relationship that enables employees to customize their careers in ways that closely match their career objectives, taking into account their life circumstances at any given point—current or anticipated. For employers, MCC creates competitive advantage in recruiting, retaining, and developing a deeper talent pool and, in turn, for achieving long-term business objectives.

MCC encourages adaptability and longer-view thinking as core competencies of both manager and employee and creates a more transparent workplace with multiple career-path options. In this way MCC addresses the business imperative to recruit and retain high-performing, high-potential employees in the intensifying marketplace for talent. It is the bridge for companies to move away from traditional corporate-ladder thinking to a more pragmatic, adaptive lattice model.

Now that you've been introduced to the many features of MCC, it's time for a look at MCC in the real world. In the next chapter, we start with an examination of three successful organizations that exhibit de facto MCC behaviors and then describe our own organization's experience in experimenting with a structured MCC approach. In our penultimate chapter, we'll build on these real-world descriptions and lessons by giving you more straight talk, this time on what it's going to take to get MCC going in your organization.

FIVE

The Journey Toward a Lattice Organization

We are, it seems, on the verge of a new world of work.

—Thomas W. Malone

Certain organizations have demonstrated a knack over the years for combining and pursuing various principles of a lattice philosophy. Their cultures reflect a number of de facto principles and systems of mass career customization. They may not have established a structured framework or a specific MCC lexicon, but the actions of these organizations speak as loudly as if they had.

The commitment to MCC-like principles and systems starts at the top with strong leaders and is executed in cultures focused squarely on employee retention and development. These organizations understand the difference between encouraging an employee's long-term career development through a sequence of jobs matched to both skills and personal life situations versus simply accommodating one-off concessions to avoid or delay resignations of valued employees.

In this chapter we look at three such examples—SAS, Arnold & Porter, and Ogilvy & Mather—that have put these principles into action and whose current leaders are evolving latticelike cultures to build further on long-running business success. We then describe the initial journey within Deloitte to implement a structured MCC program.[1]

SAS: RETAINING THE INTELLECTUAL CAPITAL

SAS is the world's largest private software company. It entered 2006, its thirtieth year in business, with ten thousand employees and the prospect of another record-setting year of double-digit revenue growth, to about $1.9 billion. SAS also has been cited often as a progressive innovator in work-life integration programs and family benefits.

These two factors—sustainable business growth and progressive employment policies—are positive preexisting conditions for creating corporate-lattice organizations, but they are not prerequisites. Organizations with sustainable growth and progressive employment policies continually create new roles, new career opportunities, and new dial-up/dial-down options. Many companies in this situation, including SAS, prefer to fill these new positions with current employees who are already familiar with the business and the company's way of doing things.

SAS is a healthy business. Based in Cary, North Carolina, the company excels in the fastest-growing product segment of the software industry—business intelligence—which it engages as part of its wide-ranging product portfolio in data-mining and analytics software. (The acronym *SAS* is derived from "statistical analysis software," the products that continue as its core business.) Customers—like Harrah's Entertainment, the casino operator—use SAS software to segment mounds of data, for instance, to identify the most profitable customers, customers who might be about to leave a competitor, and so on.[2] And chances are that SAS software is employed somewhere in your organization as well.

SAS also has a reputation as a desired employer. SAS receives two hundred applicants for every job opening posted on its Web site. Indeed, the company mainly hires experienced people—often those in their forties and fifties who have been caught in the boom and bust cycles of the high-tech industry and are particularly attracted to SAS's stable workforce. This mix of a growing business, appealing career opportunities, and workplace policies that make talent retention a strategic business priority puts SAS in an elite league. Jeffrey Pfeffer, professor of organizational behavior at the Stanford Graduate School of Business, estimates that SAS saves $60 million to $80 million a year because of its unusual consistency in retaining employees.[3] SAS has a low turnover rate, averaging just 3 percent a year in an industry where 20 percent turnover is typical. It also is tremendously efficient at retaining customers—98 percent stick with SAS year after year.

SAS believes employee continuity is a valuable selling point, especially when competing with rivals for new accounts. "Over the years, I've learned how employee loyalty leads to customer loyalty, increased innovation, and higher-quality software," says James Goodnight, CEO and founder.[4]

The case of SAS's Kecia Serwin shows Goodnight is not just speaking in clichés.[5] A self-described hard-charging sales executive, Kecia was promoted rapidly after joining SAS in 1990. Late in 2002, at age thirty-seven, she was named general manager for U.S.

commercial sales in a new internal start-up, the health and life sciences business unit. In four years she helped drive sales from a low base to more than $110 million, assembling a sales team of more than eighty people in various regional offices. Total annual revenues accelerated by 14 percent in 2006 after gains averaged between 8 and 10 percent in the previous three years. This was an achievement worthy of the classic high-performing, high-potential leader. And Kecia worked hard for it, putting in seventy-hour weeks, often spending eight to ten nights per month away from home to build the business, giving up multiple vacation days, and never taking a sick day. When she and her husband, a sales engineer, celebrated the birth of their first child in April 2005, she was away from work just ten weeks, six on official maternity leave and another four on vacation.

Yet after her return to work, Kecia soon faced a major, unanticipated crisis in her family. Early in 2006, six months after her maternity leave, both her stepfather and father were diagnosed with terminal cancer. Her stepfather died that March. At that point, with her father's condition worsening and Kecia herself still adjusting to the demands of being a first-time mother, she decided to step off her fast track entirely, for an indefinite period. "Something had to give," she recalled. "There just wasn't enough of me to go around." Kecia said extensive planning in advance of her open-ended leave included naming the leader of her team's strategy group, Kurt Kaliebe, as her interim replacement.

Just as Kecia was about to step aside, in April, her boss resigned unexpectedly, and senior management reporting lines were reorganized. Suddenly, Kecia found herself a direct report to CEO Goodnight. Would she need to renegotiate the terms of her leave? If he rejected them, would she have to consider leaving SAS? The matter was settled quickly and reassuringly for Kecia when the two executives talked it over. "You do what you need to do and come back when you are ready," Kecia said Goodnight told her. Five months later, after her father's death, Kecia and Goodnight met again. "I'm ready to come back and give SAS 100 percent," she told him. "Where do you need me?"

His answer? Right where she had been, leading the health and life sciences team. It was certainly a good outcome for Kecia, but what about the strategy specialist, Kurt, who had filled in effectively for Kecia for the previous five months? He continued reporting to Kecia and stayed in a managerial role heading one of the regional sales teams. The role provided Kurt more responsibility, more visibility, and more leadership opportunities than the strategy position. This suggests another important feature of MCC environments. When an employee dials down, it creates opportunities for colleagues to step up. In Kurt's case, five months as Kecia's interim replacement created a bridge to a new leadership role and career path that otherwise might not have been possible, or at least not possible as quickly.

In terms of an MCC profile, had she had one at the time, Kecia's would have reflected a complete dial-down in Workload during her leave (see figure 5-1). It would then reflect a partial dial-up after her return. She also informally set new Location/ Schedule limits for herself: fifty-hour workweeks and minimal travel, perhaps a week per month. Today, she says, "I have more control over my schedule." And she has begun to consider whether a more limited or part-time workload would better fit her evolving career-life fit needs when her daughter enters school in another four years. Kecia says: "My current thinking is this is what I'll need to do to meet my goals to spend more time with my daughter. I'm not opposed to working a 9-to-5 job where I can be productive while at work as an individual contributor or in management yet leave it

FIGURE 5-1

Kecia's MCC profile stages

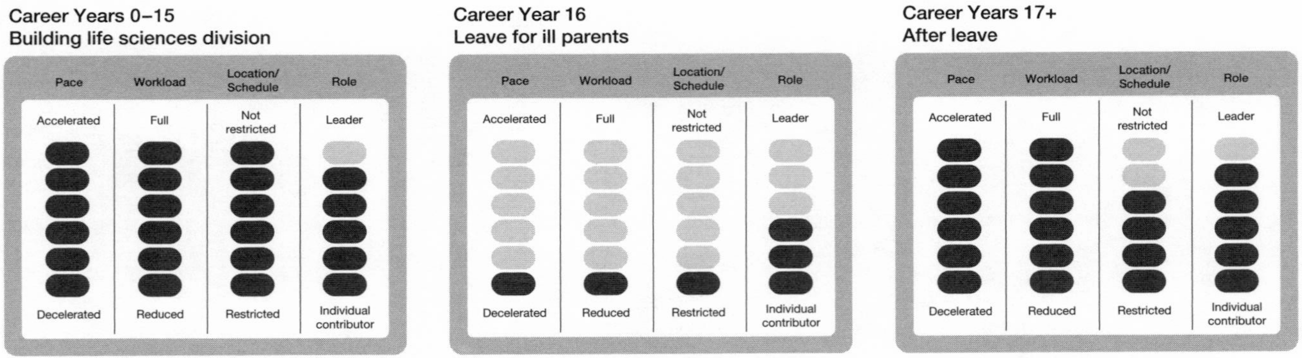

Career Years 0–15
Building life sciences division

Career Year 16
Leave for ill parents

Career Years 17+
After leave

at the office when I go home. Personally, I think that's the new challenge and/or opportunity facing today's companies. Taking the longer view really is a good way to run a business. It's also the right way. We know it's a competitive workforce out there. All things being equal, wouldn't you rather work for a company that cares about you, not just in a given job at a given time, but over the course of a full career?"

Jeff Chambers, SAS's vice president for human resources, recognizes the potential power of MCC for unifying what is still an ad hoc approach in his company. A more formal MCC system "is something we're looking at really, really seriously," he says. "We need to retain the intellectual capital because you can't replace that."[6] Chambers elaborated on this point as a panelist at the Chief Human Resource Officer Executive Forum, a conference held in 2005: "One of the hallmarks to our success is we don't really have stagnant career ladders where you go from [software] developer levels 1, 2, and 4. People move around the organization pretty freely, and we encourage that. That's one of the reasons why they grow, develop in their jobs, acquire different skills, and become more integral and important to the business. They're more well-rounded."[7]

ARNOLD & PORTER: CLIENTS VALUE CONTINUITY

Arnold & Porter is a venerable corporate law firm, perhaps best known for its world-class antitrust and corporate defense practices. Based in Washington, D.C., the firm also gets high marks for savvy counsel in the halls of the U.S. federal government. Several former senior officials of the Federal Reserve Board, the U.S. Securities and Exchange Commission, and the departments of state, justice, and the treasury are counted among its 630 attorneys.

To those who work there, Arnold & Porter is prized as one of the most desirable employers in the U.S. legal profession. The firm has been on *Fortune* magazine's annual list of the "100 Best Places to Work" for four consecutive years. In 2006, Arnold & Porter was the only law firm to make both the *Fortune* list and *Working Mother* magazine's "100 Best Companies" honor roll.[8]

There are good reasons for this. Arnold & Porter has been at the forefront in adopting an array of flexibility options for its lawyers. On any given day, forty to fifty lawyers (or roughly 7–8 percent of the firm's legal staff and twice the industry average of 4 percent) are working part-time, on temporary leave, tele-commuting, or participating in flexible work schedules or other nontraditional pacts that keep them connected in myriad ways to their full-time professional colleagues and the firm's clients. Rather than falling off the partner track, however, these associates are, in effect, dialing up and down in a latticelike path to partner and beyond. (The firm has partners as well as associates who have worked schedules other than full-time ones.)

Notes James J. Sandman, managing partner and overseer of Arnold & Porter's flexible work programs from 1995 to 2005: "It's been obvious to us for years that a culture with different career-path options helps in attracting and retaining the best talent."[9] He said what has been true for more than thirty years at Arnold & Porter is going to become even more valuable going forward for most knowledge-driven organizations.

"The forces that are increasing mobility across all professions, in addition to work-life fit, are only going to become more power-ful," he says, citing the competitive environment for talent that is pulling lawyers away from law firms and into other sectors inside and outside the legal profession. "If you can't make some progress in dealing with the work-life fit trigger for career change, you're just going to be overwhelmed." Sandman sees the ability to offer varying Pace, Workload, Location/Schedule, and Role arrangements that fit attorneys' individual professional and personal situations as a way to build loyalty: "There is an increasing attenuation of the sense of loyalty and commitment of employees to employers, in part because employees don't think that employers reciprocate the loyalty. So employees say to themselves, 'Why should I commit myself to you when I don't know if I have any future here and might be laid off in a few years?' They would like to be loyal, but they don't want to be chumps. And they want some sense that loyalty is going to be reciprocated. Those kinds of feelings, I think, run throughout the economy."

Sandman acknowledges that the firm's success in this area is tied to leadership. In his ten years as managing partner, he raised and supported the business case for career-life fit policies among fellow partners as well as in public forums. This included describing success stories of people "who have been retained and added great value to the organization as well as the cost of failure—people who left because they weren't able to make it work and how our clients and the firm as a whole are worse off for it."

Sandman's commitment to cultivating loyalty among his lawyers is mirrored in the loyalty of clients. This might seem counterintuitive. Don't clients discourage anything less than the 24/7, anytime, anywhere access to their attorneys? "Quite the contrary, some of the biggest fans of our program are clients working directly with their part-time lawyers," he says. "They like their lawyer. Clients place a high value on continuity of service. They hate to lose the person they've invested in. It turns out that a part-time lawyer isn't that much different from a full-time lawyer working on multiple client matters. How many clients really have access to 100 percent of the time of the lawyers they work with? Very few."

OGILVY & MATHER: RECOGNIZING THE NEEDS
OF INDIVIDUALS

Ogilvy & Mather, one of the world's largest marketing communications organizations, counts Cisco Systems, Motorola, and American Express among its banner clients. Ogilvy's brand-building programs have made it a perennial award winner in global advertising, marketing, and public relations.

Shelly Lazarus says creative talent has always been *the* defining ingredient for competitive advantage in marketing communications. "The people having the creative ideas are priceless," she says.[10] Now more businesses are pursuing an edge in creative talent as innovation and continuously redesigned work processes have become essential for success in global markets.

"If we used to live in a world where people would have to conform to the needs and routines of the organization, we are now in a world where the organization is going to have to recognize the needs of the individuals they want to keep employed," Lazarus says. "The war for talent is never over. You never have enough talent."

Ogilvy's tradition in developing leaders is to hire people early in their careers, giving them a variety of roles and responsibilities to season them in the Ogilvy way, as opposed to recruiting senior executives. By the time they are promoted into managing director roles, Lazarus says, most Ogilvy leaders have participated in hundreds of discussions regarding the career progression of hundreds of coworkers.

In MCC terms this means that employees building successful careers within Ogilvy have frequent, ongoing conversations with both supervisors and team members that certainly include longer-term discussion about Pace, Workload, Location/Schedule, and Role. Many Ogilvy executives have made lateral, dial-up/dial-down moves over time on the Ogilvy lattice, Lazarus adds. The bigger point, she says, is that all employees understand from the role models around them that they will have an option to dial down or temporarily move out of the agency if personal issues arise. "They know in their own minds that if they needed to do something differently, we could probably work it," she says. "That's a very, very important message for me to send to everybody."

Indeed, Ogilvy's employees have a wide range of choices among the four career dimensions. "I can't even catalog anymore the number of different work arrangements we have," Lazarus says. "We have lots of people who do odd things. We have people who have moved to other places. People who work from home one day a week, and it's not always the same day. People who need to take leaves and then come back. You can't even predict where they will need the flexibility. The only criterion is, given the needs of the individual, is this arrangement workable in light of what is required to deliver for our clients?"

Like SAS and Arnold & Porter, Ogilvy has elements of a lattice-like culture. It has eighteen thousand employees in more than 120 countries. This requires expertise for operating in a staggering range of local cultures, nations, and ethnic groups. Geographic dispersion complicates the communications challenge for Ogilvy on behalf of clients. And for Lazarus it raises the question of how and when to bend Ogilvy's business culture to retain master communicators in these cultures without compromising quality standards for its clients. How does she manage this? By consistently reinforcing Ogilvy's policies to value each individual through its strong, decentralized culture.

"As the leader, I have to be extremely conscious of where we cross a line," she says. "I'm maniacal about consistency. I care about consistency of values, philosophy, approach, and culture." Lazarus sees giving managers the ability to customize options as key. She refused, for example, to endorse a proposal floated by Ogilvy's financial staff to reduce office lease expenses because the change would have required *all* employees to work at home at least one day a week. "Leadership is really about understanding how the choices all fit together," she says. "We allow people enough freedom to work in the way that fits their needs and that fits their lives. Most people work in the office, in the cities where they live."

These three organizations are examples of enterprises built on the conviction that building long-term relationships with employees—especially high-performing, high-potential talent—is an essential plank in any platform for growing a business. Each would say that long-term client relationships are a key to profitable growth and that employee loyalty is a key to long-term clients.

While these three examples demonstrate the benefits of de facto MCC, we believe that adopting a formal, systematic approach to replacing the corporate ladder with the corporate lattice will create more consistent, scalable, and longer-term benefits that are not necessarily dependent on leaders to understand and drive this result. The profound shifts occurring in the workforce must be met with an equally transformative response, one that provides an already emerging approach for operating at two levels simultaneously: how work gets done and how careers are built.

DELOITTE'S JOURNEY

With more than forty thousand partners, principals, and employees; offices in ninety cities within the United States and its Indian operations; and revenues of nearly $9 billion in 2006, Deloitte &

Touche USA LLP and its subsidiaries (or "Deloitte") form one of the world's largest professional services organizations.[11] Deloitte is recognized as an innovator in employment practices, especially in expanding opportunities for women, minorities, and other groups.[12] Since Deloitte has a partnership structure, twenty-eight hundred partners and principals agree on strategic direction and vote on key leadership roles.

For Deloitte, the journey down the path toward MCC had its roots in its Women's Initiative, launched in 1993 by then CEO Michael Cook. His vision was a place in which everyone achieved his or her fullest potential and rose through the organization. Even though Deloitte was hiring men and women at the entry level in roughly equal numbers and investing heavily in training both along the path to partnership admission, women were leaving at a much higher rate. This gender gap in attrition, then at 7 percent, was expensive in two ways. First, with turnover conservatively estimated to cost the equivalent of twice the departing employee's annual compensation, the gender gap was costing Deloitte millions of dollars a year. Second, this leaky pipeline made it hard to keep up with the demand for services, let alone grow.

Most Deloitte leaders—both men and women—assumed that the women who left were motivated primarily to stay at home for family reasons and didn't sign on with competitors or pursue different careers paths or other lines of work. They interpreted the ongoing departures by women simply as a fact of life, not a business issue.[13]

"To be frank, many of the firm's senior partners, including myself, didn't actually see the exodus of women as a problem, or at least, it wasn't our problem," Douglas M. McCracken, then chairman, wrote in an article published in 2000 in the *Harvard Business*

Review. He added, "We assumed that women were leaving to have children and stay home. If there was a problem at all, it was society's or women's, not Deloitte's. In fact, most senior partners firmly believed we were doing everything possible to retain women. We prided ourselves on our open, collegial, performance-based work environment. How wrong we were, and how far we've come."[14]

In assessing the root causes of the gender gap in employee turnover, Deloitte learned several key lessons. The first was that women were leaving for career reasons as much as, if not more than, they were for family reasons. Over 70 percent of the women who had left were working full-time someplace else within a year, and another 20 percent were working part-time.[15] "Most women weren't leaving to raise families," McCracken noted. The second was that men were as concerned about work-life issues as women. Leaders "were surprised to find that young men in the organization didn't want what older men wanted," he wrote. "They weren't trying to buy good enough lifestyles so that their wives didn't have to work." Rather, both men and women said that they "weren't willing to give up their families and outside lives for another $100,000."

From the beginning, the organization positioned the Women's Initiative as a business strategy, meaning that it was built on a solid business case. The results prove the efficacy of that approach. The percentage of women partners, principals, and directors accelerated from 5 percent in 1993 to 21 percent in 2006, several percentage points ahead of the nearest competitor among the Big Four firms.[16]

Also in 2006, 32 percent of all new partners, principals, and directors were women; 35 percent of all senior managers were women; 38 percent of all managers were women; and the gender turnover gap virtually closed.[17]

Jim Quigley, immediate past CEO of Deloitte & Touche USA LLP, reinforced this link between Deloitte's success and the Women's Initiative. "Imagine Deloitte without our Women's Initiative," he wrote in the 2005 annual report for Deloitte's Initiative for the Retention and Advancement of Women. "We would be a much smaller organization. We would be a much less profitable organization. We would be an organization whose future would be limited."[18]

Since its beginnings, the women's initiative has focused on several issues: personal and professional development, mentoring, and helping employees balance the multiple commitments in their work and personal lives. Deloitte's 2006 Global People Commitment survey, which enjoyed an 84 percent response rate, ranked the organization highly on achieving flexibility and choice, defined as "create a culture of flexibility that respects our people's need to manage multiple commitments and providing work/life support and flexibility."[19] The culture by and large encourages a level of day-to-day control by employees over many aspects of how work gets done. One partner describes it like this: serve your clients well and be accessible when you need to be, but have the ability to take care of your personal needs. A tax manager, commenting anonymously in a 2003 survey, added: "As long as you get your work done, where you get it done and when is up to you." This informal flexibility improves retention, according to 96 percent of managers surveyed in 2003.[20]

In addition to informal flexibility, Deloitte has offered formal FWAs for over ten years. More than a thousand employees have participated in these programs, some like Tina (whose story is discussed in chapter 1) rising through the ranks while on a series of FWAs. Tina had four FWAs over eleven years that spanned two maternity leaves and required multiple reduced Workload situations ranging from 70 to 90 percent of maximum. She was admitted into the partnership in her eleventh year.

Despite these formal and informal approaches, career-life fit continues to be a struggle for both men and women, according to the 2006 Global People Commitment survey. Women made it their top priority overall in answering what the "organization can do to better strengthen its relationship with you," and men ranked it third. In addition, other internal surveys of FWA supervisors found that Deloitte partners and principals wanted more advice on how to manage the trade-offs associated with various options. It would help "if I understood how salaries are adjusted if the part-time employee significantly exceeds their hours," wrote one partner. "Clearer guidelines should be established regarding an employee's expectations for career progression and promotion when on a reduced workload," wrote another. The lack of a unified approach also meant that some people might have wanted to customize their path but didn't see a way to do it. Or they tried and failed, sometimes resigning in frustration. In other words, Deloitte's FWA program suffered from the same problems covered in the "Straight Talk About FWAs" section of chapter 3.

SYNTHESIZING THE FLEXIBILITY DATA

In 2004, Deloitte's women's initiative went through a refresh effort, resetting its vision and agenda for the coming years. Internal and external research collected as part of this effort led to a clear conclusion: flexibility was *the* top issue affecting women in the workplace. The clarity of the message was striking, and it touched off a new round of more focused research. That effort resulted in a series of interesting conclusions, among them:

- An inventory of FWA programs turned up a surprising sixty-nine various work-life programs, though anecdotally no one seemed to be able to name more than three such programs. Clearly, there was a communication problem, but it was more than that. There was an inverse relationship between the continually growing number of flexibility programs and the slight decline in satisfaction, year after year, over a five-year period. So it was clear that simply adding more arrangements to the already vast menu of options was not the answer for strengthening the organization's approach to career-life fit.

- Partners and principals stated they were supportive of FWAs, yet the number of them willing to take FWA employees onto their client engagements was limited. Put another way, they weren't walking their talk.

- Yet the demand for FWAs was higher than at any earlier point—and rising. If career-enhancing opportunities for the growing number of employees seeking FWAs could not be created, the potential for escalating turnover would be high.

- The method most widely used for accommodating the FWA requests at this time was taking qualified client service staff "off the line," or away from any activity tied directly to client projects, and placing them in internal staff-oriented roles. There were reasonable arguments in many cases for doing so, but overall this practice was not a workable solution. With 80 percent of the organization in direct client service roles and 20 percent in staff roles, the decision to move FWA employees into staff positions from revenue-generating, client-facing assignments simply wasn't scalable.

• Some of the most talented employees were leaving the organization for positions in industry. Many of them were quite satisfied with the organization. They enjoyed the culture and
were learning, growing, and developing as professionals. But
they couldn't see how to fit their career-life fit aspirations into
future roles within Deloitte down the road. So they left the
organization in anticipation of flexibility issues downstream.
In essence, they said in exit interviews, "I know how it works
for me today, but I don't see how it will work for me in the
future when my needs change."

• The feedback from employees about FWAs was divided into
two camps. As noted in chapter 3, in a series of thirteen focus
groups conducted during the fourth quarter of 2004 and the
first quarter of 2005, roughly 50 percent of those who were
actively participating in FWAs or who previously had been
participating in one said that these arrangements were working for them. The other 50 percent felt strongly that their
arrangements were not working well for them.

• Surprisingly, whether or not the respondents believed their
current arrangements were effective, virtually *all* stated that
the arrangements did not address the broader issue of their
future career paths. "My career is in no-man's-land," one
employee said. "My future is nebulous," said another—a
sentiment shared by many.

So Deloitte faced four indisputable challenges: (1) the flexibility conundrum needed to be solved; (2) demand among employees for flexible arrangements of all types was high while demand
among client service teams for FWA employees was low; (3) the
existing practice of putting FWA employees primarily into inter-

nal roles was not scalable; and (4) FWAs did not address an employee's career path and trajectory. It was clear that a fundamentally different approach to the problem was necessary.

The organization turned to the world of consumer products for a transferable model. The simple question that sparked this solution: if you can customize jeans or sneakers, then why couldn't you customize careers? Borrowing from the basic concepts of mass product customization seemed a logical approach for a radical shift, a step-function change, in how Deloitte could conceptualize and manage career development and progression. There was no compelling reason not to try. As Barry Salzberg, current CEO of Deloitte & Touche USA LLP, said, "Let's figure out what is non-negotiable like values, integrity, independence, skills, and quality, and everything else becomes a choice."[21]

FROM CONCEPT TO EMERGING REALITY

From its inception in 2004, MCC has been introduced and tested in various forums, most notably through implementation pilots within Deloitte Consulting LLP ("Deloitte Consulting"). Why start in the consulting business rather than any of the other three businesses (audit and enterprise risk, tax, and financial advisory services)? Because, in short, consulting was the most difficult business to tackle. It tends to be the most travel intensive, office locations are geographically dispersed, and the workload can be the least predictable among all the businesses. A proposal can arrive unexpectedly or a project swiftly won—and consultants deployed with little notice. These assignments occur in cities and towns across the country and sometimes, indeed, around the world. Although a consultant's preferences for being assigned within specific geographic regions are always among key factors in staffing decisions, specialty skills and related criteria required to meet a client's needs are also high on the list.

Project deployment can be for as short as a few weeks—or for as long as several years. Each project is different, so demands on the workforce on any given project vary widely. Says Cathy Gleason, the Deloitte Consulting principal leading the MCC pilot activities: "Consulting was a natural place to start. If MCC falls into place here, then it will likely fall into place elsewhere within our organization."[22]

Deloitte started the MCC pilots in Consulting for another very practical reason: its leaders were very willing participants. They recognized the changing demographics, the narrowing supply of well-qualified knowledge workers, and the increasing needs of the company's workforce—both men and women—for more elasticity and options in the employee-employer relationship.

As in the other businesses, Deloitte Consulting operates as a matrix organization. While each professional has a "major," such as an industry or service area specialty (strategy, technology, etc.), most also have secondary reporting relationships. Goal setting, career planning, development, performance evaluation, deployment, and related activities often take place at the intersection of these multiple organizational groupings. In addition, each professional has a reporting relationship with his or her project leader while assigned to the particular client account.

Project leaders (often principals) naturally have significant influence on project-level assignments and on opportunities for a consultant's professional growth within the scope of activities available on a given project. Yet career planning and development for consulting employees, for the most part, do not occur with project managers. They occur within the consultants' major and are delivered through designated counselors. These counselors typically have broader networks and experience than those of the people they advise, and they hold positions at least two levels higher in the organization.

ROUND 1 PILOTS: INCREASING THE SUPPLY OF CLIENT SERVICE OPTIONS

In the spring of 2005, when discussions on how to pilot the MCC framework began in earnest, the first order of business was to increase the supply of MCC-based options for client service engagements—the projects out in the field where 80 percent of professionals were assigned. (Recall from earlier in this chapter that the majority of FWAs were found in staff support roles.) Therefore, the first round of pilots focused on the client engagement level. One objective was to identify MCC options for practitioners along the four dimensions of Pace, Workload, Location/Schedule, and Role that were scalable for client service assignments. The second objective was to begin to define the resulting impact on career paths, client team interactions, and client satisfaction. A related piece of this effort was to identify creative but realistic ways to sell and manage projects with clients that would allow MCC options to be supported more broadly in the field.

Six existing client service account teams across a variety of industries, from financial services to health care to pharmaceuticals, were chosen in part because the principals leading them were both well regarded and generally progressive in the area of talent management. The goal was to engage these principals as early adopters and vocal sponsors of MCC. A total of 113 participants representing all staff levels, geographic regions, and service specialties were included in the six-month pilots, beginning in August 2005. Pilot managers worked with project leaders and human resources to design the tools to collect key metrics for the pilot, as outlined in figure 5-2.

FIGURE 5-2

MCC Round 1 pilots: Metrics and measurements

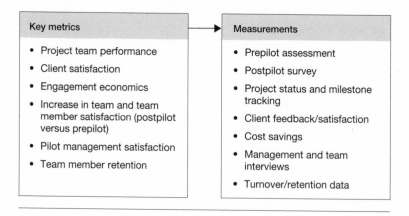

The results from the initial pilots were very encouraging and in some ways surprising. For one, none of the practitioners asked to dial down in Workload (except for two people who were on FWAs prior to the pilots and wanted to continue with their current arrangements). Another surprise was how the MCC framework was effective at the project level. It encouraged participants to have conversations about how work gets done as well as clearly provided individuals with options along the four dimensions.

Survey scores measuring satisfaction with work-life integration among these same pilot participants rose from 68 percent in the prepilot survey to 73 percent in the postpilot survey. (Specifically, the surveys asked practitioners whether they believed they had the flexibility they needed to manage their work, career, and personal life.) Some project groups posted substantial leaps, as high as 50 percentage points, from the prepilot to the postpilot survey results. Eighty-eight percent of the participants said in the postpilot survey that the options presented in the MCC program positively influenced their decisions to stay with the organization.

The MCC framework achieved these results, in large part, by enabling the conversation. Rather than have their commitment questioned for raising the possibility of working differently, the pilot participants were encouraged to articulate their work-life needs and to work together, as a team, to come up with how to meet those needs along with project demands. Since everyone was involved in these conversations, it eliminated the stigma and resentment that an FWA's accommodation-based approach so often generates. More important, pilot participants reported there were no negative consequences to having the conversation about adjusting one or more of the MCC dimensions.

"MCC forces you to be more proactive and thoughtful about how you manage work," notes Beth Kelleher, the principal leading the health care project.[23] She adds: "One of the things that we tend to get a little bit lazy about is managing expectations for the work as a whole or the project as a whole. MCC makes our project management better because it forces us to hold each other accountable. This gives everybody better work-life balance and also makes the project run more smoothly. People were enjoying their work more, they were spending less time on the road, and they were feeling more balanced. They also were more productive."

Raj Jayashankar, the project leader for the pharmaceutical client, described how MCC requires better teamwork and creates more transparency among team members. In contrast with the one-off and secretive nature of FWAs, "we found that MCC is a team-oriented approach," he says. "The whole team was involved. A program like this definitely increases morale because it gives team members additional options. Not everyone has a need to adjust their standard profile, but they know that if they have a personal situation come up, the project managers and the client will work with them to mitigate it. Overall, I think that was positive for productivity."[24]

The key learning here is that MCC operates both at the level of *how careers are built* and at the level of *how work gets done*. In the Round 1 pilots (see table 5-1), creating options along the Location/Schedule dimension encouraged an examination among both individuals and teams of how people can structure their time differently and work from locations other than their offices. In

TABLE 5-1

Round 1 pilot summary

Pilot specifications	• 6 client engagement sites • 113 practitioners from all staff levels, geographic regions, and service specialties • 6-month duration
Pilot objectives	• Test MCC framework within client service environment • Test the link between MCC and improved retention • Develop champions and success stories
Findings	• MCC and retention were positively correlated • Participants stated that a more positive and sustainable career-life fit was achieved • Morale and productivity improved due to greater control and choice around where and when work was performed • Client service standards were maintained throughout the pilot, indicating that MCC could be applied—and scaled—within client service • Even those with standard profiles felt they were able to increase their career-life fit due to more control over when and where work got done • MCC enables work redesign as an integral part of designing options for employees at the project level
Limitations	• Pace and role dimensions were not tested in meaningful ways: (1) pilots were not synchronized with goal-setting and performance management processes; (2) since pilots were organized around specific client projects, longer-term career planning generally took place outside the purview of the studies
Recommendation	• Conduct subsequent pilots within service specialty areas where a multitude of talent management processes—including goal setting, performance reviews, deployment, and career planning—are administered

addition, discussions about creating options along the role dimension inspired new thinking about how work can be redesigned into specific modules or distinct pieces. This, in turn, enables individuals and managers to design roles that better fit other dimensions of the individuals' MCC profiles. As you experiment along each dimension of MCC and how these dimensions interact, new forms of working will emerge. This is part of the value of the MCC framework.

Also, leaders of the Round 1 pilot teams felt that MCC put them at a competitive advantage in staffing their projects. Jayashankar explains: "The biggest thing we're going to get out of MCC is the ability to attract and keep people that we would consider high performers." Kelleher agrees: "We have to find ways to allow our staff to deliver the best that they can, and we have to find ways to keep staff who can deliver what our clients need. I think that's the biggest power of MCC."

While the Round 1 pilots succeeded in creating a greater sense of options for both practitioners and project leaders and explored how MCC operates at the work redesign level, they did not examine in much depth how the four MCC career dimensions work over time and in relation to each other to affect how careers are built. These pilots were not of sufficient duration to address these questions, nor were they linked to the annual goal-setting and performance review sessions. In addition, while Workload and Location/Schedule options can be adjusted (and were) at the project level, Pace and Role are longer-term dimensions that usually require planning and discussion beyond project-to-project workflow rhythms. The next round of pilots was designed to ensure that a customized road map to review and incorporate longer-term dial-up/dial-down options and possibilities, a core feature of MCC, would be part of each participant's experience.

ROUND 2 PILOTS: INTEGRATING MCC WITH THE ANNUAL TALENT CYCLE

To further refine the implementation of the MCC framework, the pilot team targeted the next round for a regional service area (RSA), the equivalent of a business unit. RSAs administer the full suite of talent management systems, including goal setting, performance evaluations, and project staffing. This seemed like a good fit with the objectives of the second pilot, which were (1) to understand how the four dimensions of MCC work in tandem and observe how the trade-offs among them shape each participant's career experience; (2) to indoctrinate the principals and senior managers on how to conduct MCC-based conversations about the career and personal goals of those they counsel; (3) to understand the impact of MCC on resourcing and selling work; and (4) to evaluate the impact of MCC on the client service business model. The question was, which RSA would be ideal for the next MCC pilot and how supportive would its leadership be?

Market demands for expertise in strategic positioning, restructuring, developing, upgrading, and implementing a broad array of IT services have soared over the past two decades. Deloitte Consulting's technology consulting practice was an early entrant into this market. Today it is one of the industry's leading providers of IT and related services. It, too, like its competitors, faces mounting talent shortages to deliver these services. So when leaders of the Technology Integration Service Area (TI) learned that a second MCC pilot study was planned, they raised their hands.

Rick Wackerbarth, head of TI operations in two West Coast regions, was one of those leaders. "The number one problem we had to address related to growth was attrition of our talented practitioners," he said. "That's why I was such an advocate of trying something new. Sustaining IT implementation projects can be fast paced for long periods. It's not unusual for people to reach burnout stage and want to step back. Some just get totally out of the profession—one [of our employees] even got into fish farming."[25]

In the view of the national TI practice leader, Jon Williams, FWAs had proved to be little help in retaining TI employees, especially practitioners facing burnout. Most FWAs in his practice created Workload or Location/Schedule changes that usually forced employees to leave client projects. "[The FWA] became the easier answer," he says. "It was implemented more often instead of designing a customized plan to allow for work-life balance as well as a continuing role as a consultant."[26] Other failings, in his view, of FWAs as a tool for retaining high performers were "spotty and subjective" management standards and the perception among most high performers that FWAs would damage their promotion prospects; hence, the most highly valued employees didn't consider FWAs.

The Round 2 pilot was launched in June 2006 (coinciding with Deloitte's fiscal calendar), with 270 of the TI practice's 415 employees prequalified to participate. Initially, there were two qualifying requirements were performance ratings of 3 ("meeting expectations") or higher and a minimum tenure of two years, which Wackerbarth felt was sufficient time for participants to establish a network of peers and project leaders. (These thresholds were subsequently eliminated.)

The first steps were to assess the efficacy of TI's existing approach to career planning and to determine practitioners' priority issues in terms of their career-life fit. The result? Prepilot surveys and focus group discussions indicated that career planning was relatively weak and that FWAs fell short of expectations. In summary, the Round 2 prepilot assessment revealed that:

- Career-planning discussions with counselors rarely went beyond a one- or two-year horizon. (Only one in five employees had longer-term discussions regarding their career plans and prospects.)

- Practitioners reported that one-third of client work was done independently and had potential for being conducted away from the client site, but only 24 percent of it was managed this way, resulting in the perception of unnecessary travel and overall practitioner wear and tear.

- A third of employees said they were not satisfied with how existing FWAs succeeded in creating greater career-life fit, yet most said having better opportunities to do this would be a deciding factor in their decision whether to stay at or leave the organization.

- Nearly half the employees said they could not see how an FWA could be incorporated into their current assignments; roughly the same percentage of employees said they feared that pursuing an FWA would be viewed negatively by their supervisors and peers.

While Wackerbarth and Williams were staunch supporters of the MCC pilot, most of the principals in TI were not familiar with the MCC framework. They had a myriad of questions about how the work could be delivered successfully while meeting client and marketplace demands. The Round 2 pilot team held group discussions and one-on-one conversations with principals to discuss their concerns about MCC and to brainstorm solutions. While some of these principals saw the value immediately, many were skeptical, asking questions including:

- If employees have options to reduce workloads, restrict travel, and so on, won't MCC just open the floodgates for schedule variations and the like, disrupting client staffing requirements?

- Won't economic and productivity objectives for the TI practice be more difficult, if not impossible, to achieve?

- How does this differ from programs we have in place today?

- What is unique about MCC, particularly when we consider what is already being done for our top performers on an informal basis?

- Wasn't MCC another well-intentioned but classic setup for failure and disillusionment? (Skeptics recalled a rapidly derailed effort several years back that purported to allow consultants to adjust schedules and design their careers. The consensus view was that it raised expectations among consultants that principals could never meet.)

The "floodgates" concern turned out to be misplaced. When the Round 2 participants were asked what MCC options were most appealing to them, many responded that they wanted to *dial up* Pace, regardless of what that meant in terms of Workload and Location/Schedule. "Especially for Gen Y, it's all about accelerate, accelerate," says Cathy Gleason. "They say, 'I may still opt out later, but by then I've gotten further along. I've gotten further faster.'"[27] As a result of this finding, counselors were coached in their Round 2 training sessions to advise fast-track employees to be clear in their expectations of what it takes to get to the next promotion level and to ensure that an accelerated path would not cause burnout.

Another message was to caution employees against overreaching when setting aggressive performance and promotion goals. "My advice to a newly promoted manager, for example, was to set a three-year goal for her next promotion, not a two-year goal," Gleason says. "Three years is still a fast pace, but it allows more room to exceed performance goals. If you are ahead of track for three annual evaluation cycles, it's a lot better than being labeled as behind on a two-year promotion track."

What impact did MCC have on the RSA profitability and talent model? The results to date from the Round 2 pilot have been consistent with those from the Round 1 pilot: no negative career impact, no visible impact to client delivery, and a positive impact on the business from savings in higher productivity and reduced travel costs. (See table 5-2 for a summary of the Round 2 pilots.) Morale increases, though difficult to quantify, are encouraging. Participants have expressed relief. They say TI leadership is acknowledging the personal trade-offs associated with the consulting lifestyle and is working on a sustainable solution.

The longer-term benefits from shifting to the more sustainable pace and travel schedule are trending positively for both the employee and the organization as a whole. All of this was accomplished without any decline in client service standards. In addition, since one of the pilot objectives was to incorporate MCC into planning projects, principals have begun to reframe expectations relative to the way work will be delivered. To date, they have found that clients are receptive to these discussions since it is common that they, too, are experiencing the same workplace-workforce tensions. In fact, clients are looking closely at Deloitte's solution with an eye toward adopting it within their own organizations.

A major objective of the Round 2 pilot study was to establish a competence among managers to initiate and conduct MCC-based

TABLE 5-2

Round 2 pilot summary

Pilot specifications	• 270 practitioners from regional Technology Integration Service Area • Participation threshold: (1) performance rating of average or above; (2) two years' tenure • 12-month duration
Pilot objectives	• Test all 4 MCC dimensions simultaneously across the performance management cycle • Test the link between MCC and business results, including retention, productivity, and cost • Develop champions and success stories
Findings	• Improved productivity, employee satisfaction, and morale due to greater choice around where and when work is performed. (More people are doing more work away from the client site—up from 24% to 29%) • More consistent and robust career conversations, cited as more satisfying by both practitioners and managers • MCC is highly valued with two-thirds of pilot participants projecting that it is likely they will need to customize one or more MCC dimensions over the next five years • Achieved significant improvement (56% compared to prepilot survey) in employees who feel they have the support they need to manage their career-life fit • Maintained client service standards; clients reacted positively to MCC approach to staffing (and were interested in hearing about pilot results) • Positive correlation between MCC and retention
Limitations	• Coordination with scheduling resources was hampered by lack of information-sharing platform • Moving from FWA-based "exception" mentality to MCC-based "new normal" mentality requires persistence and constant communication • Limiting participation, particularly based on tenure, created a feeling of "haves" and "have nots"
Recommendation	• Conduct additional pilots within other functions to prove the model for each business unit

conversations with study participants. Within the MCC framework, keeping employees continuously engaged in meaningful roles with the organization while also supporting employee-specific sine wave variations over time are key elements for success. "The worst case for us is when people say, 'I'm happy, but I'm going to leave now because I might miss out on all these other opportunities coming my way,'" says Gleason. "Just having more and better conversations between supervisors and counselors about long-term career options is one of the biggest benefits in MCC."

Although two-thirds of TI practitioners had career-planning discussions with their counselors, only one in five had comparable conversations before the Round 2 pilot. "We've made it clear we expect counselors to *initiate* these conversations now," Gleason says. "This clearly is an issue we must solve," says Jon Williams. "I'm optimistic that all the efforts surrounding this MCC pilot are helping us to learn as leaders in the organization, as well as . . . all our people to understand that it is a sign of strength, not weakness, to explore these issues. People who are not happy or are challenged in their professional life, as it relates to their personal life, are not as productive as they can or want to be."[28]

The MCC framework supports these career conversations by giving them a structure and lexicon—starting with identifying the four career dimensions and acknowledging the interplay among them. Participants in the Round 2 pilot easily accepted the end-point definitions for each of the four dimensions, but they pushed for more description of the middle nodes on each continuum. Both principals and staff said these definitions would help them clarify choices during career conversations and also better communicate a sense of fairness in establishing options and possible trade-offs.

To respond to this request, the pilot team defined choice points along each continuum (see figure 5-3).

While it is still too early to measure the longer-term impact of the MCC framework in terms of participants' careers, there clearly has been improvement in the quality of career conversations. In

FIGURE 5-3

Example of points on the continuum: Workload

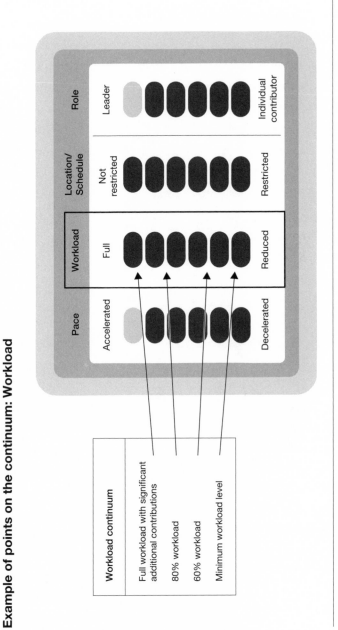

fact, the pilot team added "quality of career conversations" as a metric to measure MCC's midterm impact. Another benefit is the psychic reward to participants in knowing a model exists that systemically provides options, whether or not those options are ever exercised in an extraordinary way.

In summary, Round 1 pilots focused at the project level and showed not only that MCC can work in client service but that MCC operates at the work redesign level as well as the career-planning level. Round 2 pilots were designed to build from this core understanding, demonstrating the value of building MCC profiles for everyone in the practice group. Table 5-3 compares the design of the two pilots in terms of what each was able to test.

TABLE 5-3

Comparison of pilot design for Round 1 and Round 2

Round 1: Project-level pilots	Round 2: RSA-level pilots
• Career is executed at the project level but is owned elsewhere in the organization, limiting ability to impact Pace and Role	• Career ownership lives within RSA, so pilots can impact/measure all career dimensions (Pace and Role through career management; Workload and Location/Schedule through deployment)
• Success of career customization depends on ability to bridge divide between service area and project leaders seen as early adopters of MCC and therefore resources for other partners interested in experimenting with MCC	• Pilot projects selected through pilot RSA leadership, ensuring greater integration across talent management processes
• Complex matrix structure with limited access to full suite of professional stakeholders (counselors, geographic leaders, etc.) curtailed the scope of pilot	• Leverages existing RSA structure (geography, human resources, deployment, counseling, etc.) to integrate MCC into complex matrix structure
• Since each project has unique characteristics, customized materials were needed that made it difficult to develop/test repeatable project-level materials	• Since each service area is organized similarly, pilots at the RSA level are readily scalable across other parts of the business

THE NEXT STAGES OF THE DELOITTE JOURNEY

Capable leadership, of course, is essential for every transformational effort. Cathy Gleason was handpicked to lead the Round 2 pilot because she had more than twenty years as a high-performing consultant, had led Deloitte Consulting's West Coast practice, and also had at one point taken a leave of absence for personal reasons.

Jon Williams presents a different profile. He pursued admission to the partnership as rapidly as he could, a pace that strikes him now as unnecessary. "When I look back on it now, I wonder if it was the best idea," he says, with wry understatement. He continues: "It seems like I had a hundred years of my career left once I got there. It's easy to say that now, but it wasn't easy to think that way then. We need to help everybody understand that customizing the journey is a necessary and important part of each of our career paths. It does involve balancing. There are trade-offs with every decision, and making those trade-offs should be part of a normal career progression, not a negative thing."[29]

In addition to the pilot leaders, an MCC steering committee composed of senior Deloitte leadership was assembled. Its purpose is to promote and advocate the MCC framework among all levels of the organization's leadership and management groups. In turn, these leaders and managers are counted on to carry the torch of MCC throughout the organization. "Part of our charge is to engage the hearts—not just the minds—of the leadership and management of our organization," says Joe Echevarria, deputy managing partner of Deloitte & Touche USA LLP and member of the MCC steering committee. "The rest are sure to follow, if they're not already ahead of us."[30]

One of the primary motivations for additional pilots is the growing realization of the potential MCC creates for competitive advantage in recruiting and retention. This is true for the increasingly limited pools of new hires off college campuses and highly experienced recruits. "The fight for people with experience and talent is intensifying," says Frank Piantidosi, CEO of Deloitte Financial Advisory Services (FAS). "I'm already in the middle of it, so I know we had better be the best in the game."[31] Piantidosi signed up all eleven hundred FAS employees to participate in an MCC pilot.

Owen Ryan, senior partner and leader of Deloitte's capital markets service line, made the same decision for his group. Ryan said he believes MCC will improve both talent integration and talent retention. Both are major strategic priorities, in part because his business unit is competing for high performers with industries that are also in the midst of a talent shortage.

Ryan grew the capital markets business largely by recruiting professional experts, many with advanced degrees in engineering and mathematics. These experts represent many nationalities with various cultural and ethnic backgrounds. "When you spend time with them, you realize quickly that 'not everyone is like me,'" Ryan says. "MCC is a novel way to connect with our people. If our turnover goes down and our people are happier, then our bottom line will improve. I believe that."[32]

Interestingly, while Deloitte is moving ahead, socializing MCC across various and distinct lines of business via more pilot studies in rapid succession, its chairman, Sharon Allen, is raising a different point: should the company continue to temper the pace of full-scale MCC adoption by rolling out more pilot studies? As Allen asks the question: "There is no doubt that we are moving in the direction of MCC, so why not just roll it out universally?"[33] The organization's response, so far at least, is to continue to roll out in stages, fine-tuning and garnering support and buy-in along the way. But Allen certainly does have a point—one that should be revisited often.

We've seen in this chapter examples of three enterprises—in software, law, and marketing communications—that have informally, and intuitively, built a latticelike model into successful organizational structures and processes. These cases underscore our conviction that de facto MCC is already happening all around us. The activity is more evident in enterprises that understand—as do SAS, Arnold & Porter, and Ogilvy & Mather—how (1) employee loyalty is closely linked with long-term customer loyalty to the brand; (2) how clients value continuity of service from professionals they come to know and trust; and (3) how consistency in values, philosophy, approach, and culture are keys for building these long-term relationships.

We've also seen how another enterprise, Deloitte, has evolved over the past few years in its pursuit of a more formal, scalable MCC structure. This journey began with the discovery of a looming problem: the coming clash between employees' mounting interest in FWAs and the organization's inability to scale one-off commitments either way (dialing up or down) within its core client service businesses. MCC's major appeal, in the eyes of many participants in the pilot studies, is precisely where FWAs have proved to be weakest. MCC provides an ongoing process for employees to *customize* and *visualize* their career paths *over time* among a defined set of options that management can synchronize to fit the enterprise's strategic priorities.

SIX

Facing Forward

Sage Advice from the Front Line, to the Front Line

The value of an idea lies in the using of it.

—Thomas A. Edison

icrosoft Chairman Bill Gates once advised executives, "Don't let yourself be lulled into inaction" when thinking ten years into the future. He added, "We always overestimate the change that will occur in the next two years and underestimate the change that will occur in the next ten."[1] It's a sage warning for today's companies that have grown accustomed over the past fifty years to abundant talent pools. Pioneers who see the proverbial writing on the wall are moving to create strategic and competitive advantage to distinguish themselves in the eyes of the talent they need to attract and retain.

While it is true that informal MCC is already going on all around and that the realities of the tightening talent market will force organizations to respond in some fashion, MCC is a large-scale transformation that requires vision on the one hand and long-term commitment and attention to detail on the other. Simply tinkering at the margins won't do.

MCC is no different than any other innovation. It is going to require years of exploration and experimentation to truly understand and realize its full potential. This is because we tend to walk into the future backward, perhaps wanting to go in a new direction but not realizing that we are defining the new direction relative to our past experiences. Here's an example from everyday life: we'll call it the "TiVo revelation."

If you've installed TiVo (or a competing digital video recorder) in your home over the past few years, you can likely relate to the simple ways in which this technology is changing your life. You may have first viewed TiVo as some slick VCR that allows you to record and store TV programs digitally at the press of a button. Then you may have realized that you could record one show while watching another. Next you may have discovered that you can get a "season pass" that automatically records your favorite shows whenever they are on and then realized that you can also search for shows based on topics or actors. Eventually, you may have found the value in transferring shows to your laptop.

Further along the adoption curve, with your favorite shows stored on your laptop, you redesign more convenient ways to view and enjoy them. You find, for example, that you are no longer sitting around waiting in real time for NBC's declared "Must See TV" on Thursday nights; instead, you are watching *The Office* on Friday morning as you wait to board a flight at San Francisco International Airport. Looking back, you come to appreciate how TiVo affords a whole new way of experiencing television via a customized approach of how this entertainment tool can work best for you. (We guess you could call it "mass television customization"—but that's another topic altogether!) Similarly, with MCC you're likely to find that once you start experimenting, a whole new world of possibilities opens up.

MCC is born out of the reality that today's workforce is highly nontraditional while today's workplace is not and that demand for talent will outpace supply for the next twenty or so years. Adoption of a latticelike model is, in many respects, acknowledgment that the organization is at an inflection point relative to how it views and manages talent. "*People first* is the absolute must strategy when talent demand exceeds supply; this is how it will be for the rest of our careers," says one young boomer executive.

Having said that, we are well aware, just as in our simplistic TiVo example, that efforts at change need to start by meeting people where they live today. We work in the real world, too, and recognize that people-related strategies routinely are perceived by line managers as nice-to-have, feel-good programs. Most will focus on these programs only when they have time available to give to them (which, of course, is rarely), since the urgencies of operational needs overwhelmingly trump the "people stuff" on any given day.

Leading your organization to adopt MCC—in spirit or in form—will require a solid understanding and buy-in of the urgency regarding the supply-and-demand dynamics of the people part of the shareholder value equation. In other words, you need to answer this question: "Why should *I* care?" using the language and discipline of business.

This chapter offers guidance on how to enlist MCC pioneers through a compelling business case and then provides some straight talk about taking those first steps forward in full view of where the journey leads. We draw from years of experience in implementing transformational change, from primary and secondary research (including conversations with hundreds of people describing myriad points of view about all that MCC touches), and from what we have learned firsthand from our own implementation and analysis.

TRUE NORTH

To build a compelling business case, you will need to anchor it in the facts—and possible futures—of your organization. The workforce trends discussed in chapter 2 provide useful fodder, but you will also need to do some homework. How have the demographics of your organization's workforce changed, and how are these trending? Which talent-market trends are affecting your business, and what impact do they have? How scarce is critical talent today and what are your projections for how scarce it will be in the future? What are the competitive pressures? And so on.

Taking an enterprise value map (EVM) approach to respond to these and related questions may be useful here. The EVM is a visual representation that illustrates how shareholder value is generated, allowing executives to link strategies, initiatives, and other business activities to growing shareholder value. The main components of enterprise value or levers of value creation—revenue growth, asset efficiency, operating margin, and expectations—can be used to facilitate analysis and provide an effective way to frame and communicate the MCC business case (see figure 6-1) in bottom-line business terms.

The EVM can be a useful tool to help determine, associate, and communicate how the effects of workforce trends—and, by extension, MCC—translate to the bottom line and continued health of the business overall. For example, your business may be

FIGURE 6-1

Illustrative MCC enterprise value map

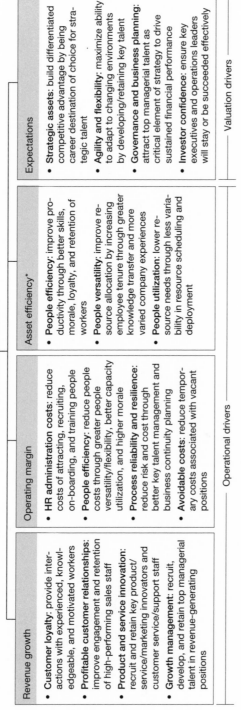

Shareholder value

Revenue growth

- **Customer loyalty:** provide interactions with experienced, knowledgeable, and motivated workers
- **Profitable customer relationships:** improve engagement and retention of high-performing sales staff
- **Product and service innovation:** recruit and retain key product/service/marketing innovators and customer service/support staff
- **Growth management:** recruit, develop, and retain top managerial talent in revenue-generating positions

Operating margin

- **HR administration costs:** reduce costs of attracting, recruiting, on-boarding, and training people
- **People efficiency:** reduce people costs through greater people versatility/flexibility, better capacity utilization, and higher morale
- **Process reliability and resilience:** reduce risk and cost through better key talent management and business continuity planning
- **Avoidable costs:** reduce temporary costs associated with vacant positions

Asset efficiency*

- **People efficiency:** improve productivity through better skills, morale, loyalty, and retention of workers
- **People versatility:** improve resource allocation by increasing employee tenure through greater knowledge transfer and more varied company experiences
- **People utilization:** lower resource needs through less variability in resource scheduling and deployment

Expectations

- **Strategic assets:** build differentiated competitive advantage by being career destination of choice for strategic talent
- **Agility and flexibility:** maximize ability to adapt to changing environments by developing/retaining key talent
- **Governance and business planning:** attract top managerial talent as critical element of strategy to drive sustained financial performance
- **Investor confidence:** ensure key executives and operations leaders will stay or be succeeded effectively

—— Operational drivers ——

—— Valuation drivers ——

*Although asset efficiency is technically a "hard asset," balance-sheet-driven concept, we have taken the liberty of applying asset efficiency principles to human assets to show that "return on assets" ideas apply well to talent management.

Source: Adapted from Deloitte Enterprise Value Map.

on a high-growth trajectory with ambitious plans, but the talent market is supply constrained for the technical talent you need. Here, the limiting factor to growing the business (revenue growth) and ensuring confidence in the company's ability to execute its strategies (expectations) will indeed be workforce issues.

Another timely example of how workforce trends may affect the bottom line is the impending brain drain risk due to the large number of boomers in senior management positions (and the ranks) who are about to retire. The loss of key management from the sales organization, for example, is likely to impact sales success (revenue growth), while the loss of key manufacturing and services managers may threaten production and support efficiency (operating margin). MCC can help you develop appealing roles to entice aging talent to extend their tenure and, at the same time, promote more effective knowledge transfer and business continuity within your organization.

To further strengthen the tie between MCC and employee retention, it helps to be able to articulate who is leaving your organization and why. Do you have the highest turnover at the lowest levels or at midlevels? Does it vary by gender or other diversity categories? Are people leaving because they recognize they have limited potential for further opportunities within your organization? Are too many of those who leave the rising-star performers counted on to drive and execute your strategy in the coming years? What is the cost of replacing them—and how likely is it that their replacements will raise similar issues of concern or discontent? Do you know at what threshold the voluntary churn of your high-performing, high-potential employees results in a minimal or even negative return on your investments in human assets? The answers to these questions are key elements of the business case, and when they point to higher-than-optimal churn rates and escalating costs, it is time to begin thinking through a systemic response—since the costs of waiting likely will not increase linearly but exponentially.

Tangibly determining, concretely articulating, and continually reinforcing how talent-market trends are likely to directly impact your business performance will help your leaders and line managers enlist and commit to the solution (*commit* is the operative word)—and not just for the first few steps, but for the whole journey. Our experience is that, despite the best of intentions, large-scale efforts like MCC simply will not be successful without unwavering executive sponsorship *and* buy-in and commitment from the line (which links to the expectations lever in the EVM). This is why we can't overemphasize the importance of the business case in creating your burning platform for implementing MCC.

So think of your business case, conveyed through an EVM lens, as an all-encompassing prerequisite for establishing "true north," the raison d'être for relentlessly pursuing MCC. Be sure to factor in the broader business context and to communicate how your bottom line is being—and is expected to be—affected by impending workforce constraints. Along the way, be sure to focus particular attention on the following three actions: casting a wide net, making it real, and conquering skepticism with success stories.

Casting a Wide Net

In your quest for bottom-line benefits, think broadly about how MCC can improve the efficiency of your operations. For example, as you implement MCC, you may invest in work redesign that presents more choices about where, when, and how work is done. These choices can lead to significant operational benefits, from business continuity to real estate costs and beyond, driven at least partly by MCC. After the 9/11 attacks on the World Trade Center in Lower Manhattan, many companies were forced to relocate large segments of their workforce to neighboring states. Many invested heavily in the types of information communications and technology equipment that create more options in deciding how and where work gets done.[2]

Similarly, soaring real estate costs coupled with new communications and other enabling technologies have prompted many companies to examine how greater mobility and remote-work arrangements can improve their employees' productivity and reduce requirements and costs for office space (see the Sun Microsystems case in chapter 2). MCC gives you a compelling reason to move in this direction.

Making It Real

As we said at the outset of this chapter, large-scale trends are not always salient or visible to line managers, especially those in frontline operational roles who are rightly focused on "now" rather than "what's next." So it is important that MCC speaks to them directly, at the level of their day-to-day experiences.

For example, ask your line managers to add up how much time they spend trying to fill positions with top talent. The answers will surprise many. Countless managers have stories of how it took months to fill key openings, how others had to work longer and harder to fill the gap, and how these vacancies created a mountain of work that simply didn't get done. These situations can take a heavy toll on both operating performance and people. To make the business case real, connect these episodes back to the big picture. Ask your managers to recall all the various one-off arrangements they are *already* managing, and then have them count how many more requests for flexibility are being tendered. Tying these commonplace events together makes it easier to see that they are not isolated but rather related data points along a worsening trend that requires a systemic response.

Once workforce trends are connected to managers' daily struggles, the next step is to connect the solution to MCC. Some leaders will understand the power of MCC quickly. Others will be more skeptical and will need a chance to voice their doubts and disagreements. Welcoming their concerns and investing the time to address them creates some level of buy-in. As noted in the previous chapter, the leaders of the MCC pilots spent a lot of one-on-one time talking with fellow principals who were skeptical. By investing this time, the pilot leaders were able to not only convince the skeptics that, at a minimum, "business as usual is not an option" but to ultimately enlist their buy-in to deliver the MCC message further along the line.

Conquering Skepticism with Success Stories

Since MCC is already going on informally in many organizations, if you look around, more than likely you will find success stories—managers who have been employing MCC principles—with great results. Highlight these stories. There may also be leaders in your organization whose careers have followed an MCC-like path, leaders such as Gary in chapter 4 or Kecia in chapter 5, who at times dialed down in one or more dimensions and later dialed back up. Recognize these as examples of how the organization is already operating in an MCC-like fashion. Providing such illustrations as proof that the shift to a latticelike model is already under way helps diminish the understandable angst that some may initially feel about making a significant change in talent management practices. Keep in mind, also, the sizable adjustments in attitude and mental models that you are asking managers and leaders to make all along the way.

In addition to collecting success stories, have managers and leaders fill in their own MCC profiles. As we discuss in the opening and closing chapters, everyone in your organization (including yourself) already has an MCC profile. It's just likely that no one thinks about it in these terms at a conscious level. Instead, people quietly assume that everyone else must have made their way up singularly by climbing the traditional corporate ladder. Understanding all the different choices that are represented in the people around you will make MCC seem less revolutionary and more evolutionary.

Thus each of these three points—casting a wide net to make the business case compelling and exhaustive; selling the case to other senior leaders and midlevel managers in ways that inspire buy-in and commitment; and overcoming resistance through success stories drawn from early wins and informal MCC role models within your organization—is required to help your organization pursue its "true north" for sustaining and growing enterprise value.

Your organization is sure to face several challenges during the course of its transformation to a lattice organization, so we focus the remainder of this chapter on another round of straight talk—this time on MCC—aimed at highlighting the key elements for effective adoption.

STRAIGHT TALK ABOUT MCC

"There are no priorities among essentials" is wise counsel officers and professors give to future army leaders enrolled at the United States Military Academy at West Point.[3] We are mindful, given our own experience, that there will be pitfalls that could derail MCC from delivering on its potential. In that spirit, we explore here what we consider the most likely hazards, and solutions, so you have some idea of what may lie ahead.

Consistency Doesn't Necessarily Mean the Same

We have said all along that MCC will evolve in different ways in each organization. The four career dimension endpoints, and perhaps even the career dimensions themselves (though less so), should be calibrated specifically for your organization. For example, what is considered a full workload in your organization? For professionals in knowledge-driven organizations, it may be a range of hours that realistically reflects workload demands of various positions. This range of hours may even be composed of both core requirements and adjunct expectations (such as recruiting, office morale activities, involvement in community programs, and so on). Be sure to craft a tailored definition for each dimension.

In tandem with these tailored definitions, the endpoints along the continuums will also need to be set in collaboration with each business unit. This allows for the fact that career paths and expectations, as well as constraints, may differ based on the nature of the business or function. You'll need to find a workable balance between (1) conformity across business lines that both simplifies the operational side of MCC and talent movement across organizational boundaries and (2) tailoring the framework to meet the specific needs of various organizational units. A general rule of thumb is to keep the dimensions the same across the organization but, if and as warranted, to tailor the endpoints of each dimension to reflect the specifics of each unit's operations. Strict organizational conformity is not a requirement (this is mass career *customization* after all). The MCC framework is designed to be highly adaptive and, within reason, tailored to the circumstances of specific businesses. Adoption will be better if approached in this manner.

Although this may seem like an arduous task, many organizations won't be starting from a blank page. In general, setting dimensions and endpoints is a fairly intuitive exercise that is best led by individuals who are most knowledgeable about the workings of the business. (In chapter 5, we described how and why the Round 2 TI pilot team defined the endpoints—and several points along each continuum.)

It Goes Both Ways

To achieve the benefits of MCC, you'll need to provide for movement along each dimension. If options along any MCC dimension are a dead end in the sense that an employee can't go back to a previous profile setting, they won't work. For example, along the Pace dimension, you will need to think through how to allow people to accelerate as well as decelerate (a learning from Deloitte's Round 2 pilot). You will also need to allow people who have decelerated to resume a normal pace, or to even accelerate pace, in the future.

Similarly, in the Role dimension, it would be helpful to support people moving from one department or function to another—and back. This could mean moving from a line to a staff position and then going back into line work. Some organizations today are not open to supporting lateral movement while others (think General Electric) consider it a core competence. Still others are open to cross-organizational movement but have few (or no) processes to help employees identify suitable roles across the organization. In short, creating a new lattice mind-set may also require some level of process and infrastructure to support this kind of internal movement.

Taking this one step further, you may want to also consider ways for your people to go in and out of your organization, not just in and out of roles or up and down on Pace and Workload. For example, Deloitte has a program, called Personal Pursuits, that allows employees who meet a tenure and performance threshold to terminate their employment *but stay connected* in ways that keep their professional networks current and active for up to five years. Activities include continuing coaching and mentoring relationships; maintaining eligibility for professional and skills development programs; ensuring that professional accreditations are kept current; and, often, even receiving invitations to annual holiday parties. This support is ongoing—so long as the former employee doesn't sign on with another employer.

For the individual enrolling in the program, Personal Pursuits is an answer to the hardest part of opting out of the workforce with the intention to ultimately opt back in: staying current and connected. For Deloitte, Personal Pursuits provides a pool of experienced hires who know the organization well and whom the organization knows well. And for current employees, it provides option value—the comfort in knowing that, if needed, they can step out of the workforce for a period and then step back into the organization.[4]

Encouraging talented people to stay active in your organization, even if they step out for a while as productive contributors, positively impacts the four levers of the organization's value drivers.

MCC Is About Enabling, Not Entitling

As with most things new, it will take a while for the lattice organization to find its "center"—that is, understand what MCC really is and, equally important, what it is not. A misperception can arise when individuals misinterpret MCC as an entitlement program and adopt a view that it gives them license to set their own rules— without consultation or consideration of their job requirements and the business's needs.

To the contrary, in both spirit and form, MCC is a career *enabler*. It enables careers in multiple ways, including opening up new possibilities about how careers are created and sustained; making transparent both the choices and associated trade-offs; and retaining talent by cultivating a new sense of loyalty and connection. While

MCC shifts the relationship between employer and employee to a collaborative one, it doesn't postulate that "anything goes."

This misperception cropped up in the Round 2 pilots. In this case, several junior employees (who were just learning the rules of work) erroneously concluded that MCC essentially gave them carte blanche to decide various aspects of their jobs. Our counsel on this: be clear about (and communicate often) the intention of MCC and set the level of expectations. Being cognizant of, and vigilant about, the entitlement inclination of some during the change process will help keep this overly zealous bunch in check.

MCC Has Its Own Language

We trust that we've made it abundantly clear by now that MCC is not just for women, nor is it just about work-life issues. We have observed, however, that there is a natural tendency for people to associate MCC too closely and too narrowly with flexible work arrangements and work-life issues, generally in the tone of "flex on steroids." This is unfortunate because MCC is an *evolution* from FWAs and not an extension of them and because thinking of it in terms of the latter leaves a whole lot of value on the table. (Recall from chapter 3 the shortfalls we described in "Straight Talk About FWAs," including that they oftentimes are accommodations to an immediate personal crisis and are too often career dead ends.)

We encourage you to draw as much distance as possible between current FWAs and MCC as a more structural solution so that your mental model can more readily shift without taking the baggage of FWAs along with it. Language has proved to be a powerful tool in this regard. We've paid close attention throughout this book, for example, *not* to use the word *flexibility* in relation to MCC. We do think flexibility is a good thing (and even a good word), but it's important to be as clear as possible that MCC is fundamentally different from FWAs. So instead of flexibility, we prefer to talk about options, choices, adaptability, and elasticity—and about career-life fit rather than work-life balance. These changes may seem subtle or small, but their cumulative impact can make quite a bit of difference.

Time Is of the Essence

It is only fair to acknowledge that MCC is a high-touch proposition. It requires a significant commitment of time on the part of leaders and managers to get to know their employees, to engage in meaningful career conversations, and to seek out and craft options that work for the business and for the individual. It is not something that can be accomplished with a ten-minute conversation once a year. A check-the-box approach to MCC will minimize its impact.

MCC gives you the structure, but you also need to make sure that you give managers the right incentives to invest the time it will take to do MCC right. If you think you can't afford to make this investment, it is time to revisit your will to change. When you look at the effect of converging talent trends through the EVM lens, the truth may well be that your organization can't afford *not* to.

Trust Is of the Essence, Too

Ambitious, talented people want to work at a company that takes their careers seriously and will provide a wide range of exciting opportunities over time. Business leaders have told us, "I need as many people as possible who not only are ambitious but also want to realize their ambitions *here*, in this group, in this company." And employees have said through surveys we've reviewed, "Showing an interest in my career development at a more personal level through strong mentoring relationships is the most valuable thing the company can do to strengthen its relationship with me."

If we're honest about it, even when managers freely give the time, not all of them are good at listening and thinking about what is best for the employee (and, therefore, the employer), especially in the holistic sense of integrating career, work, and life. Early on, many managers and employees may be ill at ease, even uncomfortable, articulating their full intentions and constraints, and we admit, we can't blame them. This is pretty new territory for everyone. What are employees comfortable sharing? What questions are managers legally allowed to ask?

While a big part of MCC's value proposition is improving discussions about careers paths and trajectories in general, through both practice and a common language, this will not necessarily happen by itself. Rather, you will need to educate both managers and employees about how to have these conversations. The upside? MCC will help differentiate you in the talent marketplace. Additionally, it will promote stronger loyalty over time by emphasizing a personal, customized relationship between your organization and your employees.

Part of the Whole

Earlier we established that MCC needs to be integrated into your varied talent management processes. This is because, at its heart, MCC provides a framework to reposition nontraditional, nonlinear career paths as business-as-usual occurrences. Applying MCC requires moving beyond the notion that nontraditional paths are based on one-off exceptions. Moving beyond this notion, however, also requires that MCC not be viewed as a separate, isolated program that stands apart from routine career conversations.

In our experience, the most critical integration points for MCC are with goal-setting, performance management, compensation and benefits, and succession-planning systems. There are additional integration points of value as well. Workforce planning, scheduling and deployment, and training and development are some other notable points of intersection. Just as in the TiVo example above, over time your organization will see *new* possibilities for reexamining—and even reinventing—a full complement of talent management and operational processes.

Success Is Relative

Talented, ambitious people want to be recognized for their contributions, even if they are not always dialed up across the board. Employees understand that compensation is relative to workload—for example, a 75 percent workload means you are compensated at 75 percent of a full salary. But they don't understand why their performance ratings are downgraded automatically (either through policy or through common practice) if they chose anything other than continuous full-time employment.

Be sure to evaluate performance on a *relative* scale—that is, whether this person performed exceptionally *relative to his or her current goals* (which should be aligned with his or her MCC profile). Without this calibration, the benefits of MCC will be marginalized. For many, it's not a matter of money as much as it is a matter of recognition for commensurate contribution.

At the same time, it will be tempting to view MCC as a benefit or reward for your high performers. While establishing eligibility criteria allows you to target the MCC framework to those segments of your workforce with the highest value to you, doing so also runs the risk of disenfranchising employees who may be the most in need of adjustments to the standard. It is critical to separate performance issues from MCC decisions. One way to achieve this, for those at the low end of the performance spectrum, is to give managers the discretion to deny to poor performers those choices along the MCC dimensions that confer greater autonomy and rewards.

The Full Measure of Success

Because very little will stay constant once you embark on the MCC journey, you cannot expect to measure the success of MCC in single before-and-after snapshots. Rather, the full measure of its impact will be cumulative—over a long period of time. The ultimate measure of success will be whether people with different MCC profiles thrive and rise in your organization over time because MCC fundamentally is about changing the ways careers are built.

Since careers aren't built in a day—or even a year or so—you will want to design the metrics that will best track how well MCC is taking hold. Early on, one gauge may be how many leaders and line managers sign up to experiment with MCC. Another one, which surfaced in the Round 2 pilots, could be the quality and frequency of career conversations. Is the MCC framework fostering more robust conversations? Do your managers feel they have the right language and information to enter these conversations with growing confidence? Do your people feel they are getting what they need and being heard?

As your organization progresses on the MCC journey, another metric is the level of "people commitment" reported in internal employee surveys. Do people report feeling more connected and committed to your organization? Have you converted those who are ambitious and eager to engage into employees who want to succeed and engage *at your company*?

With respect to retention, are you keeping more of your top performers? And to what extent are work-life issues receding as prominent factors in exit interviews and other data provided by departing employees? Conversely, are your recruiting costs decreasing? Are you attracting higher-caliber talent than before due to the differentiating power of MCC? How has it helped build your brand in the talent marketplace?

Since a more dedicated workforce should also result in more direct operational metrics—like higher customer satisfaction and loyalty, for example—it is important to measure these as well. Remember that the EVM can be a useful tool in this regard.

Robert Frost was a retired teacher when he first started to write poetry. When one of his students asked him why he tried something so different from what he had done most of his life, he replied, "Because people believed in me ahead of the evidence."

At some level, you will have to commit to MCC with this same spirit and conviction. Believe, then profit, ahead of the evidence. We are confident and trust that by now you agree that a decade's worth of evidence on MCC-led impact lies just over the horizon. Ten years from now, we believe, corporations in the knowledge-driven economy that methodically ingrain MCC principles and practices to evolve into latticelike organizations will have shown substantive business advantage in their marketplaces.

In this chapter we emphasized the importance of establishing "true north" for your organization through a specific business case that documents the relevance and significance of moving toward becoming a lattice organization. We also cataloged several likely hazards and roadblocks that will need to be overcome and outlined solutions for doing so. In our final chapter, we offer some keen examples of MCC-like thinking and activity that are transforming the workplace today and examine four major workforce challenges that we believe will be—and in many cases, already are—high on the strategy agenda of market-leading CEOs.

SEVEN

Living in a Lattice World

Nothing is so awesomely unfamiliar as the familiar
that discloses itself at the end of a journey.

—Cynthia Ozick

All organizations either adapt to change or deal with the consequences of stagnation. Change can be about the trivial things, such as the rituals of the business lunch. Up through the early 1980s, for example, employees often were expected to linger with clients over three-martini lunches; few organizations today would think to mandate their employees' liquor consumption with valued clients (except perhaps to forbid it!).

Or change can be about the big things, such as technologies that impact how, where, and when people work. When the Internet first became accessible to people in the mid-1990s, many companies saw it as a distraction and resisted giving their employees access.[1] Today few global companies deny their knowledge workers access to the Internet, even as they struggle to determine where the boundaries of access should be drawn.

Companies that do more than simply adapt, that ride the leading edge of change rather than trailing behind it, are in the best position not merely to survive but to thrive. We have made the argument throughout this book that changes in the demographics of the workforce, the shift toward a knowledge-driven economy, the structure of family life, the evolution of enabling technology, and the nature of work itself are challenging the firmly rooted corporate-ladder model of career progression.

The signs are all around us: Generation X and Y men whose workday is defined by the day care center's hours; women who step out of the workforce and then step back in doing something different from what they did before; college graduates who have no qualms about quitting their jobs to pursue personal adventures and then returning to the workforce ready to pick up where they left off. Not only is each of these forces gathering strength on its own, but they are converging and producing a profound disconnect between the nature of the *workforce* and the structure of the *workplace*.

We believe that a corporate-lattice model of career progression is emerging as the new way to structure the workplace to fit the workforce. The lattice structure, by definition, allows movement in varying directions and can be repeated at any scale. In our application, a latticelike construct allows employees to move in different directions as they build their careers, not limited to the binary world of "up or out" or "on or off" that defines the corporate ladder. Faced with this either-or decision, too many high-performing, high-potential employees step off the ladder—and take their training, knowledge, and experience with them. And, as we explored in chapter 3, stepping back onto the ladder is difficult for all involved.

In contrast, the corporate lattice opens alternative paths for high-performing, high-potential employees to not only contribute to achieving strategic priorities in the short term but to remain connected to the organization in ways that allow for greater contributions over the long term. The corporate-lattice model is centered on the practical perspective that it is easier to keep people in the system than to have them step in, out, and then back in again years down the line. It is also centered on a related insight: increasingly, the career journey in the knowledge-driven economy will look similar to a sine wave, with climbing and falling phases of employee engagement.

We have also introduced mass career customization, the framework on which to build the lattice organization. Over the past several decades, many companies have learned that personalizing the customer experience is good for business. We have extended this popular and profitable concept of defined choices to the workplace. MCC is the foundation for companies to build a new systemic credibility with their workforce. We use the word *credibility* because MCC affords a sense of transparency, understanding, and appreciation for various career paths as a business priority. We use *systemic* because, with MCC, all employees participate in a consistent process that changes today's attitude from exception and accommodation to the norm.

MCC is a discretionary, rules-bound framework designed to anticipate as well as to drive ongoing organizational change. Leading the transformation to MCC principles and practices requires vision and commitment, while the nine straight talk points discussed in the previous chapter provide pragmatic advice for success.

We agree with the many scholars who argue that designing adaptive organizations and leading them effectively is a core competence of great business leaders. "We believe that the only way to ensure that organizations will be able to change is to design them to change, to create organizations that love to change," say authors Edward E. Lawler III and Christopher G. Worley of the University of Southern California's Center for Effective Organizations.[2]

In their 2006 book, *Built to Change: How to Achieve Sustained Organizational Effectiveness*, Lawler and Worley incorporate some aspects of corporate-lattice thinking in what they describe as built-to-change, or "b2change," organizations.[3] For example, today as many as 60 percent of managers in large companies have no idea whether they are included in their companies' management succession plans; still more have no idea where they rank in these plans. Secrecy in leadership development and promotion programs fits "well in a world of paternalistic management and top-down moves," Lawler and Worley conclude, but does not fit well in more adaptive, modern organizations, where "a major advantage of transparency and openness policies" is that "they allow individuals to self-manage their careers."[4] We agree with this—and raise it one because we believe the most productive way to build careers is through collaboration between the individual and the organization.

The one-on-one conversations between supervisor and employee around the four dimensions of MCC—Pace, Workload, Location/Schedule, and Role—are the sine qua non of the MCC framework. These four dimensions provide a common language for structuring conversations about career progression and, in that way, build both consistency and transparency.

For the supervisor, these conversations also provide a regular, sanctioned mechanism and lexicon for articulating business objectives and goal-setting priorities with the employee. Moreover, MCC gives supervisors a more honest picture of their resources so that they can make better staffing forecasts and keep the overall mix of talent aligned with changing strategies and objectives.

For the employee, these conversations ensure the chance to balance work and personal life through adjustments to the MCC profile. To be sure, most employees—we estimate 90 percent or more—will have an MCC profile that reflects today's five-day, forty-hour-week standard at any given time. Yet knowing that there is a model and process for adjusting the profile as needed creates tremendous *option value*—the term we use to reference the knowledge that you don't have to fall off the career track if you need to change one of the four dimensions at any particular stage of your career.

MCC is already occurring in an informal sense in many organizations. Faced with mounting pressures from the changing workforce, managers and those they supervise have strung together a series of individualized, one-off point solutions in an effort to retain top talent and meet the needs of the business. In fact, our research is rich with examples of people who have, in effect, unknowingly created their own MCC profiles by dialing up or down. To give you a sense of the power of plotting career progression in this manner, we invite you to create your own MCC profile (and perhaps profiles for those around you). Think back over the course of your career:

- What were the stages you went through?

- How was each stage marked by different points along the four MCC dimensions?

- How did the four dimensions interrelate with each other?

We provide a blank MCC career stages profile template in figure 7-1. Take a moment to plot your own course to date—and perhaps even what you anticipate your path may look like going forward. If you're so inclined, also take a few moments to complete similar profiles for those around you, or do it together.

We venture to guess that you will be not only be surprised at the variety and richness of the MCC profiles you and those around you build, but also better equipped to have conversations with those you manage and mentor about how to consider what their MCC profiles look like today—and what they might look like tomorrow. Since career dial-ups and dial-downs are already occurring, for reasons cited throughout this work, now is the time to scale these ad hoc practices by giving them structure, scale, and, yes, even a lexicon.

EVOLVING THE WORKPLACE TO MATCH THE CHANGING WORKFORCE

As we saw in chapter 2, technology is one of six converging trends that have heightened the tension between the new nontraditional workforce and the rigid, outdated workplace structures that characterize most large organizations. From broadband to browsers, Internet-based communications and interactive media can be applied in myriad ways that create new models for the nontraditional workforce to connect in an increasingly virtual, nontraditional workplace.[5] This is especially true in global companies, where the need for new processes to encourage collaboration and raise productivity is most pronounced.[6]

Reconfiguring the Work Space

Consider Cisco Systems, the world's leading provider of network communications technologies with 2006 revenues of $29 billion.

FIGURE 7-1

MCC career stages profile template

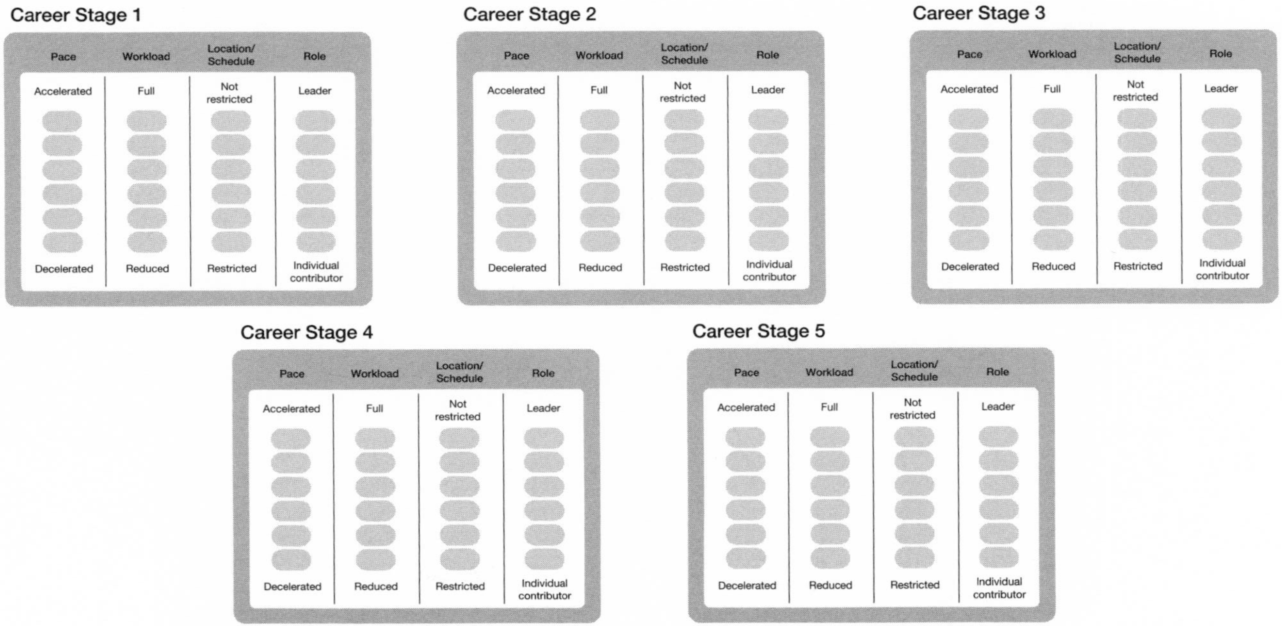

Career Stage 1

Career Stage 2

Career Stage 3

Career Stage 4

Career Stage 5

Cisco's global organization—embracing fifty-four thousand employees based in seventy countries—has for years served as a captive laboratory for re-creating and evolving the modern workplace. (For instance, its TelePresence system, an advanced videoconferencing technology introduced in 2006, was developed through testing by Cisco employees to improve long-distance collaborations.)[7]

Cisco's work effectiveness program is an example of how a workplace effort has expanded into a series of activities collectively targeted to appeal to the modern workforce. The program was jump-started amid the financial setbacks in the telecommunications industry that rocked Cisco (among many others) after the dot-com implosion in 2001. The two-part agenda—cutting costs and risk while raising productivity—quickly expanded to include a third: analyzing how Cisco employees could collaborate more effectively.

Project leaders learned early on that employees were away from their cubicles one of every three hours a day. Said another way, 33 percent of its office space was idle at any point in time, resulting in excessive office space expense. How could Cisco pare this needless overhead and improve productivity at the same time? The answer lay in the same set of facts that revealed the prevalence of empty cubicles. If employees weren't in their offices, where were they? It turns out that they were often in meetings (one-on-ones, small or large groups), away at conferences or training sessions, or on the road with clients or business partners. If the existing floor plan was not well matched with the rising number of group activities, what should replace it? The conclusion: a more open, flexible, adjustable work environment including enabling audio, data, and videoconferencing systems and even digital signage and visitor management, which was still in development at the time.

Within months Cisco's Building 14 at its Silicon Valley headquarters came to resemble a theatrical stage where props and sets changed daily. Cubicle walls came down. Open areas for group collaborations or individual laptop activities emerged, including lounge settings stocked with chairs, tables, and movable partitions. The net result? The ratio of individual to collaborative space went from 90/10 to 30/70. Conference rooms for formal team presentations remained, but smaller rooms were added nearby for groups or individuals to work independently. And so on. In addition to a 40 percent reduction in office space, operational benefits from this demonstration project included paring required IT infrastructure materials by 55 percent and cable infrastructure by 54 percent.[8]

This was, in effect, a mass customization experiment—countless possibilities within a fixed set of boundaries—for Cisco employees to personalize their office space. The results were so popular with employees that a fourth objective was added to the work effectiveness agenda: attracting and retaining talent.

Why? The positive buzz among Cisco employees spread fast through their personal networks, raising Cisco's profile as a preferred employer on campuses and with employees at competing telecom companies. Presentations and tours featuring the work effectiveness concept and accomplishments became standard elements of campus visits by prospective employees. In 2006, a fifth objective—incorporating environment-sustainability features in building systems management—was added to the mix.

Greater mobility, reduced air travel, faster response times, reduced safety risks, improved space utilization, and more extensive, nimble collaborations between team members in multiple locations were key benefits identified through Cisco's experiment to adapt its workplace to its new workforce. "This is how younger

employees want to work today," says Christina S. Kite, vice president of global workplace resources and enterprise risk management at Cisco. "They were comfortable as teenagers playing video
games and even chess with someone in Poland they met online."
Better, easier collaboration among employees, whether in the same
or distant locations, will reduce related environment demands for
water, energy, and other natural resources, which is also appealing
to Generation X and Y employees, she said.[9]

Cisco sees interest in this holistic approach to workplace effectiveness spreading quickly on a global basis. In Europe, for example, the adoption of connectivity and related technologies is
expected to create new waves of remote-work options and other
opportunities to improve work-life balance similar to those that
have already taken root in the United States.[10]

Redesigning Jobs

And it's not just the workplace configuration that is changing.
The way jobs are designed will change as well. Since 2005, Harvard
Business School's Leslie A. Perlow, a professor of organizational
behavior, has been conducting research on modularizing job tasks:
"Given the increasing number of people struggling to meet the
competing demands of work and life outside of work, the question
arises: Why are jobs defined as they currently are? Are tasks optimally allocated across individuals? Could the work be done more
productively if the tasks were reallocated among individuals?
Could tasks be divided among people in ways that are optimal in
terms of productivity but do not require everyone to have a job
that is the same 'size' in terms of work hours?"[11]

Perlow is exploring whether jobs can be segmented into many
sets of interdependent tasks an employee is expected to perform,
rather than having jobs defined based on the time allotment re-

quired. The goal is to determine whether businesses can operate in a way that enables employees to choose jobs or assignments consisting of an appropriate number of modules to suit their personal needs. "Redefining jobs based on modules would likely have a profound positive effect on both organizational productivity and individuals' ability to manage work and life outside," Perlow says.[12]

Her hypothesis, which we subscribe to, is that individuals increasingly will have less flexibility in terms of how much work they do at any stage in their career. If, instead, jobs were defined and structured modularly, organizations would likely benefit because tasks would be allocated optimally among individuals. At the same time, individuals would benefit because they could choose how many modules to take on during any given period in their professional lives.

Using Virtual Networks

And there are other evolving and converging workplace trends as well. Younger employees, in particular, already have exhibited remarkably advanced instincts for building personal networks. Technology is part of the reason, especially social-networking technologies made popular by Generation Y enthusiasts who are fearless in embracing new communications tools and online research methods. Social-networking schemes like MySpace and video-sharing sites like YouTube are having profound impact, creating added torque for tearing away existing limits of connectivity and widening opportunities for latticelike communications and career movement.

Consider what is happening at Citigroup. By the end of 2006, Citigroup had officially recognized thirty-six employee networks, such as groups focused on issues related to women; working parents; people with disabilities; the gay, lesbian, bisexual, and transgender community; and people of African, Asian-Pacific, and Hispanic heritage. There was even a multicultural network in the United Kingdom called Roots.[13] Each network was initiated by employees, and collectively more than eleven thousand employees belonged to at least one network in 2006, a 140 percent increase in membership in two years. What began mainly as peer-networking activities among Citigroup's network members evolved quickly into an unanticipated internal recruiting forum highly valued by various business unit leaders within the global financial services organization.

These leaders are eager to speak at venues such as the Learn the Business meetings that many of these networks sponsor, says Ana Duarte-McCarthy, Citigroup's chief diversity officer.[14] The meetings provide the business unit leaders forums to describe and promote their strategies, challenges, and opportunities before potential internal recruits. These events often draw standing-room-only crowds because employees are eager to learn about potential career paths. This is yet another example of lattice organizations already happening. "Employees who participate in these professional development programs have figured it out," Duarte-McCarthy says. "It's beautiful how they navigate—all driven by their desire for more information and to become involved with these networks to make it happen."

MCC is simply a more structured, evolving talent framework that taps into this desire for more information, more transparency, and wider networks. Much as mass product customization has been a hit with consumers eager for more personalized products and services, MCC creates a sense of belonging by more actively involving employees in their own career-path design—in fact, insisting on this involvement—and engendering greater loyalty along the way.

Informal MCC also is happening at Citigroup through an on-line interactive channel for employees and supervisors dedicated to one-on-one conversations about nontraditional work schedules. The program was introduced in 2005 after Citigroup surveys showed that lack of flexibility was a major employee concern. To apply for a variation on the traditional 9-to-6 work schedule, employees describe their role, how their work would be accomplished, any technology or special equipment required, and so on. They also assess likely business impact on clients and coworkers.

Employees are not asked or expected to explain the reason why they want the schedule change. (This takes supervisors out of the role of judging which reasons are appropriate and which are not.) Rather, supervisors evaluate flexibility requests solely on whether employees can continue meeting business requirements if the requests are approved. The result? More than five thousand applications came in during the first fourteen months; 66 percent were approved, 9 percent were declined, and the remainder were under review by either managers or HR staff, Duarte-McCarthy said. Thirty-five percent of the schedule-change requests came from men, yet another data point underscoring the changing attitudes of men overall.

Younger, well-educated employees entering the workplace are instinctively looking for MCC-like opportunities to customize their job progression along a variety of career paths. "They are very comfortable with virtual networks and with very broad movement both virtually and physically," Duarte-McCarthy says. "Flexibility is a core consideration of what they hope for in their careers." Some observers go further, saying many younger employees are planning their lives in distinct phases, sequentially emphasizing work, parenting, travel, and perhaps something very different. This concept has come to be known as "chunking."[15]

Creating Value in New Ways

Broadly speaking, the emphasis on greater transparency and information flows in the corporate-lattice model is aligned with the ways business value increasingly will be created in the future. Lyn Jeffery, a research director at the Institute for the Future, a think tank that advises corporations, sees lattice organizations creating more opportunities for Generation Y employees to exploit new technologies and social-networking patterns in the workplace similar to what Duarte-McCarthy has observed at Citigroup. "You can call it bottom-up leadership, or bottom-up value creation," Jeffery says. "It's the whole movement toward reorganizing the way value is created. Business value, financial value, social value are all being created in a different kind of a way, which we think will affect the way organizations work."[16]

Wikipedia, the free and most widely used online encyclopedia, is one example of volunteer-led value creation. Introduced in 2001, Wikipedia has attracted more than seventy-five thousand active contributors for 5.3 million articles in one hundred languages. Of those, 1.7 million articles in English had been created by the end of March 2007, correspondingly with "hundreds of thousands of visitors making tens of thousands of edits" daily.[17] Wikipedia is an early example of new applications in bottom-up value creation that are well suited and well timed for the emerging corporate-lattice organization. "EBay provided a platform for people to swarm, to buy things they want or sell things they want to get rid of," says Jeffery. "All of the value was created by the people who come there voluntarily. How do you lead in that kind of model, creating the conditions for innovation and success? This is something facing every organization we talk to."

Cisco's program toward increased work effectiveness is an example of reorganizing the way value is created. The company is literally reconstructing the environments in which employees collaborate face-to-face, both in person and virtually (through advancing telecommunications and audio and video technologies), which lines up squarely with the way the workforce is evolving.

The acquisition deals for MySpace and YouTube amounted to staggeringly high revenues. What might this portend for privately held LinkedIn, the largest social network aimed at business users? Perhaps a huge acquisition payday for its owners as well. According to Reuters, the number of registered LinkedIn users rose by more than 50 percent between March and September 2006, to nearly 8 million. Revenues grew twice as fast, according to a company executive, and are on a pace to reach $100 million in 2008.[18]

As workers increasingly bring consumer technologies and applications into the workplace—yes, even MySpace, YouTube, and LinkedIn—employers will have no choice but to learn how to adapt. Companies that figure it out ahead of their competitors will enjoy an edge in appealing to and retaining talented workers. Jeffery explains: "New technologies provide the connectivity, and people like doing it. People want to create their own personalized places and share it with each other. We think this is one of the big—*huge*—challenges for organizations. How do you organize your people to take advantage of what they know, what they want to do—and enable them to do it? How do you create conditions for people to mobilize around issues and projects?"

Because they promote transparency and upward movement along many paths, lattice organizations are in a stronger position to answer these questions than top-down, more unyielding ladder organizations. MCC sits at the crossroads between the traditional workplace and the nontraditional workforce we described in chapter 2. Organizations that can understand and tap each employee's career ambitions through MCC will be in a better position to attract and retain these employees and to take advantage of what their employees know and what those employees can contribute. These organizations will further benefit by more nimbly adapting their strategies to exploit what Jeffery describes as "the aggregated value of these bottom-up efforts."

MCC AND KEY CHALLENGES OF TOMORROW'S WORKPLACE

In the following section, we catalog four major workforce challenges discussed in previous chapters and describe how MCC will help business leaders address each in the coming years. We do so to underscore MCC's immediate relevance to today's C-level agenda and to offer a unifying framework that brings clarity and cohesion to what seemingly may be viewed as a disjointed set of issues. These challenges are (1) recruiting, (2) retention, (3) the leadership pipeline, and (4) leadership diversity.

Recruiting and Reentry: Accelerating Costs or a Reversal?

Leading organizations and workforce scholars, including several whose insights we've noted in this and previous chapters, have written extensively about a new consumerism in the way knowledge workers approach job searches.[19] While many employers have been slow to recognize and respond to this new sophistication, MCC provides the process for catching up. MCC extends common discussions beyond "How much do you pay me?" to "How do I continue to grow and develop?" (answer: through adjusting Pace,

Workload, and Role) and "How do I create some control over my time?" (answer: by adjusting Location/Schedule and Workload).

Indeed, early adopters of MCC should expect to see a swell of interest in recruiting efforts on campuses as college students increasingly favor a more fluid, customized organizational structure. MCC will likewise have an impact on recruiting experienced hires, especially those who have off-ramped from the corporate ladder. To date, the opportunities for reentry, or on-ramps, have been too few and far in between.

Retention: Revival or Dissolution?

A significant impact of MCC on longer-term careers is likely to be measured in retention—keeping talented employees connected to the business over the long term.[20] We anticipate that today's employee replacement costs, conservatively estimated at more than twice the annual compensation per employee and as high as five times the annual compensation in many cases, will continue to increase as the scarcity of skilled workers worsens.[21]

This may seem counter to much that is written about the rising generations and their propensity to be less committed to any given organization than the boomer generation was at a similar career stage. Actually, it's quite consistent. Most of these young to middle-aged employees (ages eighteen to forty-two) would prefer to stay in one organization, but that preference has strings attached. They prefer to stay with one employer *if* that organization reflects their values and delivers on their expectations, according to research conducted by both the Institute for the Future and Catalyst.[22]

Lattice organizations build loyalty and stability by partnering with employees to customize career paths. They build loyalty through an awareness that personal issues may take precedence over careers during certain periods—while at other times the reverse can be true. The benefits of increased employee loyalty include reduced turnover, training, and recruitment costs; wider and deeper institutional knowledge within the workforce; a deeper leadership pipeline; and more commitment to the brand and business objectives.

Leadership Pipeline: Bolstering Ranks or Gaping Holes?

Several factors will exacerbate the risk of a shortage in leadership talent. RHR International asserts that America's five hundred largest companies will lose half of their senior managers by 2010 or so, as the downsizing of the past two decades adversely affects organizations. According to the *Economist*, anticipated gaps in the talent pipeline mean that "everyone will have to fight harder for young talent, as well as learning to tap (and manage) new sources of talent."[23]

Many firms realize that reengineering, automation, and other initiatives to lower costs and raise revenues have been pushed "as hard as they can" under the cost-benefit banner raised by executives in pursuit of higher productivity, according to the *Economist*'s analysis. "Now they must raise productivity by managing talent better."[24] By increasing loyalty, commitment, and breadth of experience, MCC will deepen the ranks of aspiring, motivated leaders in organizations that pointedly position leadership development as a strategic imperative.

MCC addresses the leadership pipeline at the front end (occupied by employees in their thirties and forties) and the back end (occupied by employees in their fifties and sixties) and points in between. It helps circumvent the "gray ceiling" (discussed in chapter 1) that many younger employees see as a roadblock to promotions that could last well into the future. It also creates greater fluidity in organizational movement, which particularly benefits the younger end of the leadership pipeline continuum. (For example, see in chapter 5 how Kurt Kaliebe's opportunity to fill in as an interim replacement at SAS led to a new leadership role for him.)

On the other end, MCC has the ability to directly engage boomer employees by anticipating and activating a variety of options among the four career dimensions. These options can be calibrated for boomers' preferences, for example, to downshift in the workplace and pursue outside interests or to accelerate, such as when child rearing or elder care responsibilities are no longer a factor in their lives. This is a key imperative, given that, by 2025, the number of workers ages fifty-five to sixty-four is forecast to rise 89 percent; for those age sixty-five or above, the projected increase is 117 percent.[25]

"Increased longevity and health will encourage greater numbers of older people to remain longer in the workforce," says Ben S. Bernanke, chairman of the Federal Reserve Board. "Slower growth in the workforce will motivate employers to retain or attract older workers—for example, through higher wages, more flexibility in work schedules, increased training directed toward older workers, and changes in the retirement incentives provided by pension plans."[26]

No matter which end of the leadership pipeline is at hand, better managing the pipeline is a core objective of MCC.

Leadership Diversity: Stagnation or Increasing Numbers?

People, especially younger people, in any organization look to find role models—others, particularly leaders, whom they can emulate. However, the leadership ranks of many organizations today are highly homogeneous. MCC extends the range of role models among organizational leaders by promoting greater diversity in career paths and life choices that moderate or accelerate the pace of career progression.

For example, MCC promotes greater gender diversity as more women are able to shift the focus of their talents and energy over time between career and personal priorities yet continue to rise in the organization rather than opt out of the workforce the way 50 percent feel compelled to do today. (Recall that MCC emphasizes *keeping* people in the system.) As more leaders with diverse paths and backgrounds rise in organizations, supervisors and employees will find it more natural to explore and experiment with variations of MCC profiles.

In the strictest interpretation, MCC is a talent management framework. Yet, as these points suggest, it's ultimately about improving both hard and soft operational business measurements. Hard metrics include cost reduction (increased retention, lower recruiting and training costs); shortened learning curves, enhanced productivity, and faster innovation and time to market (deeper institutional memory, more robust collaboration networks); and improved planning and budgeting (clearer strategic alignment resulting from regular supervisor-employee MCC conversations).

Softer metrics include building an embracing yet still hard-charging culture, employee satisfaction and morale, and, ultimately, loyalty—all of which influence the more tangible metrics just listed. Viewed in this context, MCC is a multidimensional tool that both strengthens and deepens senior leaders' ability to drive continuous improvement throughout their organizations.

THE ELEPHANT IN THE ROOM

With all this said—the business challenge well articulated, the arguments convincing and defensible, and the course of action well laid out—we are aware that not everyone is on board in recognizing that (1) there is a structural workforce shift at hand, (2) the workplace must respond in kind, and (3) now is the time and place to sustainably address this challenge.

Perhaps this perspective is best described by my [Cathleen] recent personal experience in a comfortable local Italian restaurant with a great friend and newly retired mentor.[27] Over a leisurely dinner we began talking about workforce trends in general and the subject matter of this book specifically. After some good-natured bantering back and forth, his bottom line took me aback. At the end of the day, he asserted, the most successful people in business possess two qualities: they are talented, and they work really hard. (The clear inference is that anyone who had dialed down, by definition, didn't work really hard.)

As I paused, organizing my thoughts to respond to this claim, his wife, Cindy, jumped in—which was uncharacteristic when it comes to business topics. A dear friend and someone whom I admire for her many qualities, Cindy had just spent the past forty years or so being the quintessential corporate wife. She was very comfortable with her position, dedicating the "working years" of her life to this role.

"The reason that you were so successful," she interjected, "is because you had the talent and you worked really hard *at one thing*—your career. All the other elements of life during those years were handled by me." To be sure, from child rearing to household projects to domestic finances to community contributions and beyond, Cindy carried all the noncareer responsibilities. She was, in essence and reality, the not-formally-appointed COO of their household.

Cindy went on to remind her husband that this division of labor in their marriage was not so for their three married children, all in their thirties and parents of young children. She pointed to her oldest son as an example. He was talented and worked very hard—and so did his neurologist wife. The difference was that they did not work hard singularly at their careers. They worked hard as a team, traversing home and work responsibilities.

Cindy's point? The delineation between the home front and the work front has become irreversibly blurred. While she and her husband typified the 17 percent of the U.S. population that categorize the traditional workforce, their children, on the other hand, characterize the 83 percent that do not. And this was not likely to change.

With this we wholeheartedly agree. It is not likely to change. So it's time to start thinking through how to deal with this new reality structurally and systemically—and that's what this book is *really* all about.

NOTES

Chapter 1

The quotation from Andy Warhol can be found in Andy Warhol, *The Philosophy of Andy Warhol: From A to B and Back Again* (New York: Harcourt, 1975), 113.

1. E-mail message from Mike Vakili to Eric Openshaw, forwarded to Cathleen Benko by Eric Openshaw, September 11, 2006.

2. U.S. Bureau of Labor Statistics, *Women in the Labor Force: A Databook* (Washington, DC: GPO, 2005), 1; data is from 2004. Jacqueline King, *Gender Equity in Higher Education: 2006* (Washington, DC: American Council on Education, 2006).

3. Families and Work Institute, *Generation & Gender in the Workplace* (New York: American Business Collaboration, 2004), 3.

4. Ibid. See also Catalyst, *The Next Generation: Today's Professionals, Tomorrow's Leaders* (New York: Catalyst, 2001).

5. Robert J. Grossman, "The Truth About the Coming Labor Shortage," *HR Magazine*, March 2005, 49–50.

6. Ken Dychtwald, Robert Morison, and Tamara J. Erickson, *Workforce Crisis: How to Beat the Coming Shortage of Skills and Talent* (Boston: Harvard Business School Press, 2006), 6.

7. Claudia Goldin, "The Quiet Revolution That Transformed Women's Employment, Education, and Family" (paper presented at the Richard T. Ely Lecture, Harvard University, Cambridge, MA, January 6, 2006). See also Sylvia Ann Hewlett, *Off-Ramps and On-Ramps: Keeping*

Talented Women on the Road to Success (Boston: Harvard Business School Press, 2007).

8. Families and Work Institute, *Generation & Gender in the Workplace.* See also Catalyst, *The Next Generation.*

9. Kerry Daly and Linda Hawkins, "Fathers and the Work-Family Politic," *Ivey Business Journal,* July–August 2005, 4–5.

10. James J. Sandman, telephone interview by Anne Weisberg and Jenna Carl, tape recording, September 25, 2006.

11. Dychtwald, Morison, and Erickson, *Workforce Crisis,* 46–56.

12. Myra M. Hart, "Models of Success" (paper presented at the Models of Success breakfast, Harvard Business School, Cambridge, MA, May 9, 2006). Sixty-two percent refers only to that subset of Harvard Business School women who are ten, fifteen, or twenty years out (approximately thirty-five to forty-five years old) and who have more than one child. A snapshot of all HBS women would have a lower percentage of women out of the full-time workforce (influenced heavily by the much larger numbers of graduating women in the past ten years, most of whom don't yet have more than one child).

13. Margaret Steen, "Stop Out, Hunker Down, Move Up?" *Stanford Business Magazine,* February 2007, http://www.gsb.stanford.edunews/bmag/sbsm0702/feature_integration.html.

14. Deloitte & Touche USA LLP, *Flexible Work Arrangement Turnover Study* (New York: Deloitte & Touche USA LLP, April 2004).

15. U.S. Census Bureau, "Maternity Leave and Employment Patterns of First-Time Mothers, 1961–2000," *Current Population Reports* (Washington, DC: GPO, 2005). The report notes a dramatic increase in married women who had children and were in the workforce between 1970 and 1990.

16. Charles Rodgers, "The Flexible Workplace: What Have We Learned?" *Human Resource Management* 31, no. 3 (1992): 183–199.

17. Ibid.

18. Ellen Galinsky, James T. Bond, and E. Jeffrey Hill, *When Work Works: A Status Report on Workplace Flexibility* (New York: Families and Work Institute, 2004), 4–25.

19. Mary Mattis, "New Forms of Flexible Work Arrangements for Managers and Professionals," *Human Resource Planning* 13, no. 2 (1990): 138. Survey found that 100 percent of employees on part-time schedules were women and 96 percent of those sharing jobs were women. The only

flexible work arrangement that men use in any number is telecommuting. Mattis's survey showed that 55 percent of telecommuters were men and 45 percent were women.

20. Hewlett, *Off-Ramps and On-Ramps.*

21. Mary Shapiro, Cynthia Ingols, and Stacy Blake-Beard, "Optioning In Versus 'Opting Out': Women Using Flexible Work Arrangements for Career Success," *CGO Insights*, January 2007. Survey of over four hundred women in middle management found that close to 90 percent had demanded at least some form of informal flexibility from employers. The study also found that only 2 percent had insisted on an arrangement that was less than full time.

22. Anne Fisher, "Have You Outgrown Your Job?" *Fortune*, August 21, 2006, 54.

23. Ibid., 52.

24. Ibid., 52–54.

25. Lindsey Gerdes, "The Best Places to Launch a Career: The Top 50 Employers for New College Grads," *BusinessWeek*, September 18, 2006, 64–81.

Chapter 2

The quotation from Heraclitus can be found in G. S. Kirk, "Natural Change in Heraclitus," *Mind, New Series* 60, no. 237 (1951): 35–42.

1. Carol Bryce-Buchanan, e-mail to Anne Weisberg, September 10, 2006, reporting increase in media mentions of Family and Work Institute.

2. "The Search for Talent: Why It's Getting Harder to Find," *Economist*, October 7, 2006; Jody Miller, "Get A Life!" *Fortune*, November 28, 2005, 46–56; and Kelley Holland, "When Work Time Isn't Face Time," *New York Times*, sec. 3, December 3, 2006.

3. "Manpower: The World of Work," *Economist*, January 4, 2007. See also Ronald Alsop, "Ph.D. Shortage: Business Schools Seek Professors," *Wall Street Journal*, January 9, 2007.

4. Deloitte Research, "It's 2008: Do You Know Where Your Talent Is?" (New York: Deloitte Development LLC, 2004), 3.

5. The Conference Board Inc. et al., *Are They Really Ready to Work? Employers' Perspectives on the Basic Knowledge and Applied Skills of New Entrants to the 21st Century U.S. Workforce* (Alexandria, VA: Society

for Human Resource Management, 2006); data is from four hundred employers. See also Rebecca Knight, "Entrants to U.S. Workforce Ill-Prepared," *Financial Times*, October 1, 2006.

6. The Conference Board Inc. et al., *Are They Really Ready to Work?*

7. Ken Dychtwald, Robert Morison, and Tamara J. Erickson, *Workforce Crisis: How to Beat the Coming Shortage of Skills and Talent* (Boston: Harvard Business School Press, 2006), 6.

8. David Barboza, "Sharp Labor Shortage in China May Lead to World Trade Shift," *New York Times*, April 3, 2006; Diana Farrell and Andrew J. Grant, "China's Looming Talent Shortage," *McKinsey Quarterly*, no. 4 (2005): 70–79.

9. Many EU countries are also experiencing tight labor markets for skilled workers due to the loss of such employees to better markets and to fewer of them immigrating to the EU. See Joellen Perry, "Exodus of Skilled Workers Leaves Germany in a Bind," *Wall Street Journal*, January 3, 2007.

10. Robert J. Grossman, "The Truth About the Coming Labor Shortage," *HR Magazine*, March 2005, 49–50. The 2005 reduced visa supply was sapped in the first day visas became available.

11. Ibid.

12. Edward Tse, "China's Five Surprises," *Strategy + Business*, January 16, 2006.

13. Felice N. Schwartz, "Management Women and the New Facts of Life," *Harvard Business Review*, January–February 1989, 65–76.

14. Phyllis Moen and Patricia Roehling, *The Career Mystique: Cracks in the American Dream* (Lanham, MD: Rowman & Littlefield, 2005).

15. Ibid.

16. U.S. Census Bureau, *America's Families and Living Arrangements: 2003* (Washington, DC: GPO, 2004).

17. Sam Roberts, "51% of Women Are Now Living Without Spouse," *New York Times*, January 16, 2007.

18. Catalyst, Families and Work Institute, and the Center for Work & Family at Boston College, *Leaders in a Global Economy: A Study of Executive Women and Men* (New York: Catalyst, 2002).

19. Ellen Galinsky, James T. Bond, and E. Jeffrey Hill, *When Work Works: A Status Report on Workplace Flexibility* (New York: Families and Work Institute 2004), 4–25.

20. Suzanne Bianchi, John P. Robinson, and Melissa A. Milkie, *Changing Rhythms of American Family Life* (New York: American Socio-

logical Association and Russell Sage Foundation, 2006), 13–17. Relying on the U.S. Census's time-diary data from the past forty years, the authors found that men are increasingly spending more time with their children and that married fathers wish they had more time to spend with their children.

21. Catalyst, *Two Careers, One Marriage: Making It Work in the Workplace* (New York: Catalyst, 1998).

22. Society for Human Resource Management, *SHRM 2003 Eldercare Survey* (Alexandria, VA: Society for Human Resource Management Research, 2003). Data is from a self-selected sample of employers.

23. National Academy of Sciences, *Beyond Bias and Barriers: Fulfilling the Potential of Women in Academic Science and Engineering* (Washington, DC: National Academies Press, 2006), S-3.

24. Carol Evans, *This Is How We Do It: The Working Mother's Manifesto* (New York: Hudson Street Press and Working Mother Media, 2006). See also Mary Shapiro, Cynthia Ingols, and Stacy Blake-Beard, "Optioning In Versus 'Opting Out': Women Using Flexible Work Arrangements for Career Success," *CGO Insights*, January 2007; Catalyst, *Women and Men in U.S. Corporate Leadership: Same Workplace, Different Realities* (New York: Catalyst, 2004).

25. U.S. Department of Education, National Center for Education Statistics, "Table 246. Degrees Conferred by Degree-Granting Institutions, by Level of Degree and Sex of Student: Selected Years, 1869–70 Through 2013–14," Digest of Education Statistics: 2005, June 2006, http://nces.ed.gov/programs/digest/d05/tables/dt05_246.asp.

26. National Academy of Sciences, *Beyond Bias and Barriers*, 3–11; Amanda Ripley, "Who Says a Woman Can't Be Einstein?" *Time*, March 7, 2005. Ripley cites National Science Foundation figures. The article points out that women are still less likely than men to receive doctoral degrees in science and engineering. As of 2001–2002, of students receiving bachelor's degrees, women accounted for 61 percent in the biological sciences, 85 percent in health sciences, 48 percent in chemistry, and 47 percent in math. However, women accounted for only 19 percent of engineering, 28 percent of computer science, and 22 percent of physics bachelor's degrees.

27. Jennifer Delahunty Britz, "To All the Girls I've Rejected," *New York Times*, March 23, 2006. A number of letters to the editor were written in response to this op-ed piece.

28. Tamar Lewin, "At Colleges, Women Are Leaving Men in the Dust," *New York Times*, July 9, 2006. This is part of a series of articles in the *New York Times* from 2006 called "The New Gender Divide."

29. U.S. Department of Labor, "Women in the Labor Force in 2005," June 19, 2006, http://www.dol.gov/wb/factsheets/Qf-laborforce-05.htm.

30. Ibid.

31. Robin Cohen and Linda Kornfeld, "Women Leaders Boost Profit," Barron's Online, September 4, 2006, http://online.barrons.com/ article_search/SB115715054502452224.html?mod=search&KEYWORDS =kornfeld&COLLECTION=barrons/archive.

32. Ibid.

33. Linda Tucci, "Gartner: Firms at Risk of Losing Women Technologists," SearchCIO.com, December 5, 2006, http://searchcio.techtarget.com/ originalContent/0,289142,sid19_gci1233089,00.html?track=NL-162&ad =574445.

34. Catalyst, Center for Education of Women at the University of Michigan, and University of Michigan Business School, *Women and the MBA: Gateway to Opportunity* (New York: Catalyst, 2000), 36.

35. Myra M. Hart, "Models of Success" (paper presented at the Models of Success breakfast, Harvard Business School, Cambridge, MA, May 9, 2006).

36. Moen and Roehling, *The Career Mystique*, 70.

37. Sylvia Ann Hewlett, *Off-Ramps and On-Ramps: Keeping Talented Women on the Road to Success* (Boston: Harvard Business School Press, 2007), 25–55. Data is based on a Harris Interactive survey of a self-selected sample of 2,443 women and 653 men.

38. Ibid., 14.

39. Ibid., 29.

40. Ibid., 39.

41. Ibid., 40.

42. Monica McGrath, Marla Driscoll, and Mary Gross, *Back in the Game: Returning to Business After a Hiatus* (Philadelphia, PA, and Austin, TX: Wharton Center for Leadership and Change Management and the Forté Foundation, 2005). Data is from a survey of 130 self-selected participants who met profile requirements.

43. Hewlett, *Off-Ramps and On-Ramps*, 29. See also Claudia Goldin, "The Quiet Revolution That Transformed Women's Employment, Education, and Family" (paper presented at the Richard T. Ely Lecture, Har-

vard University, Cambridge, MA, January 6, 2006), 23–24. Goldin cites a study called College and Beyond funded by the Andrew W. Mellon Foundation that found that the periods when women are out of work are even shorter: "The sum of all out-of-work spells was just 1.55 years; that for women with children was 2.08 years and that for women without children was 0.41 years."

44. Evans, *This Is How We Do It.* See also Catalyst, *Women and Men in U.S. Corporate Leadership.*

45. Quotations from Hans Morris come from a telephone interview by Anne Weisberg, tape recording, October 6, 2006.

46. Robert Orrange, "Aspiring Law and Business Professionals' Orientations to Work and Family Life," *Journal of Family Issues* 23, no. 2 (2002): 287–317. Data is from interviews with forty-three self-selected law and business students.

47. Bianchi, Robinson, and Milkie, *Changing Rhythms of American Family Life.*

48. Jody Miller, "Get a Life!" *Fortune*, November 28, 2005. Data is from self-selected male senior executives of *Fortune* 500 companies.

49. Lisa Belkin, "Life's Work: Flex Time for the Rest of Us," *New York Times*, December 17, 2006.

50. Kerry Daly and Linda Hawkins, "Fathers and the Work-Family Politic," *Ivey Business Journal*, July–August 2005.

51. Families and Work Institute, *Generation & Gender in the Workplace* (New York: American Business Collaboration, 2004), 4.

52. Catalyst, *Women in Law: Making the Case* (New York: Catalyst, 2001). Study found that male partners reported the highest levels of work-life conflict of any group in law firms.

53. Ellen Galinsky, telephone conversation with Anne Weisberg, September 11, 2006.

54. Hewlett, *Off-Ramps and On-Ramps.*

55. Galinsky, Bond, and Hill, *When Work Works.*

56. Ibid.

57. Daly and Hawkins, "Fathers and the Work-Family Politic."

58. James A. Levine and Todd L. Pittinsky, *Working Fathers: New Strategies for Balancing Work and Family* (Fort Washington, PA: Harvest Books, 1997).

59. Stephanie Dunnewind, "Attitudes About Paternity Leave Are Changing," *Seattle Times*, November 19, 2003.

60. Marilyn Elias, "The Family-First Generation," *USA Today*, December 12, 2004. For more on younger generations' expectations, see Orrange, "Aspiring Law and Business Professionals' Orientations to Work and Family Life"; and Moen and Roehling, *The Career Mystique*.

61. Catalyst, *The Next Generation: Today's Professionals, Tomorrow's Leaders* (New York: Catalyst, 2001).

62. Families and Work Institute, *Generation & Gender in the Workplace*.

63. Danielle Sacks, "Scenes from the Culture Clash," *Fast Company*, January 2006. See also Anne Fisher, "Want a New Job? Give Your Old One a Makeover," *Fortune*, January 5, 2007. Article mentions a poll by the Society for Human Resource Management of a self-selected sample of employees that found that 75 percent of the employees were looking for a new job. Of these job hunters, 48 percent were searching for a job with better career development opportunities; only one-third sought higher compensation as their chief objective.

64. Ellen Galinsky, telephone conversation with Anne Weisberg, September 11, 2006.

65. Susan Eisner, "Managing Generation Y," *SAM Advanced Management Journal* 70, no. 4 (2005).

66. Ibid.

67. Larry Rulison, "Gen Y in Search of Flexibility," *Philadelphia Business Journal*, September 22, 2003.

68. Sacks, "Scenes from the Culture Clash."

69. Leigh Buchanan, "The Young and the Restful," *Harvard Business Review*, November 2004, 1.

70. These technologies include, but of course are not limited to, desktop computers and laptops, mobile phones, and PDAs, as well as software for word processing, e-mail, enterprise resource planning, customer relationship management, supply-chain management, knowledge management, business intelligence, and business process management—to name just a few applications that continue to create exciting new opportunities to accelerate productivity and innovation.

71. WebSiteOptimization.com, "China to Pass U.S. in Total Broadband Lines," October 2006, http://www.websiteoptimization.com/bw/0610/.

72. Associated Press, "For Many, Their Cell Phone Has Become Their Only Phone," *USA Today*, March 24, 2003, http://www.usatoday.com/

tech/news/2003-03-24-cell-phones_x.htm. Stefan Lovgren, "Can Cell-Phone Recycling Help African Gorillas?" NationalGeographic.com, January 20, 2006, http://news.nationalgeographic.com/news/2006/01/0120_060120_cellphones.html.

73. Thomas W. Malone, "The Gartner Fellows Interview," interview by Howard Dresner, Garter.com, March 8, 2005, http://www.gartner.com/research/fellows/asset_126360_1176.jsp.

74. Eric Richert and David Rush, "How New Infrastructure Provided Flexibility, Controlled Cost and Empowered Workers at Sun Microsystems," *Journal of Corporate Real Estate* 7, no. 3 (2005): 271–279.

75. Pamela Nicastro, e-mail to Cathleen Benko, February 7, 2007.

76. Richert and Rush, "How New Infrastructure Provided Flexibility."

77. Robyn Denholm, telephone interview by Cathleen Benko, December 14, 2006.

78. David Douglas, "Better Can Be Cleaner; Cheaper Can Be Greener: Sun's Energy-Efficient Design Breakthroughs" (presentation at Sun analyst summit, San Francisco, February 6, 2007).

Chapter 3

The quotation from Henri Matisse can be found in Edward Sankowski, "Serious Art and Autonomy," *Journal of Aesthetic Education* 28, no. 1 (1994): 31–36.

1. Mary Shapiro, Cynthia Ingols, and Stacy Blake-Beard, "Optioning In Versus 'Opting Out': Women Using Flexible Work Arrangements for Career Success," *CGO Insights*, January 2007.

2. The Ecology of Careers study is reported in detail in Phyllis Moen and Patricia Roehling, *The Career Mystique: Cracks in the American Dream* (Lanham, MD: Rowman & Littlefield, 2005).

3. Phyllis Moen and Stephen Sweet, "From 'Work-Family' to 'Flexible Careers': A Life Course Reframing," *Community, Work & Family* 7, no. 2 (2004). See also Moen and Roehling, *The Career Mystique*.

4. American Institute of Certified Public Accountants, Work/Life & Women's Initiatives Executive Committee, *AICPA Work/Life and Women's Initiatives 2004 Research* (New York: American Institute of Certified Public Accountants, 2004), 8. Data is from self-selected samples of members of the American Institute of Certified Public Accountants and partners or managing partners of public accounting firms.

5. Monica McGrath, Marla Driscoll, and Mary Gross, *Back in the Game: Returning to Business After a Hiatus* (Philadelphia, PA, and Austin, TX: Wharton Center for Leadership and Change Management and the Forté Foundation, 2005).

6. WFD Consulting, *The New Career Paradigm: Attracting and Retaining Critical Talent* (Newton, MA: American Business Collaboration, 2006), 12. Findings are for exempt men and women in the professional workforce. Data is from a Harris Interactive online survey of 2,775 self-selected exempt and nonexempt employees of medium and large corporations.

7. National Association of Law Placement, "Few Lawyers Work Part-Time, Most Who Do Are Women," December 7, 2006, http://www .nalp.org/press/details.php?id=65. Numbers are specifically for part-time options. Sample includes mostly large law firms, nearly fifteen hundred individual law offices, and over a hundred thirty-two thousand lawyers. See also Maggie Jackson, "Finding the Work-Life Balance," *Boston Globe*, June 19, 2005.

8. Catalyst, *Women in Law: Making the Case* (New York: Catalyst, 2001), 41.

9. Joan Williams and Cynthia Thomas Calvert, *Solving the Part-Time Puzzle: The Law Firm's Guide to Balanced Hours* (Washington, DC: National Association of Law Placement, 2004).

10. Ellen Galinsky, James T. Bond, and E. Jeffrey Hill, *When Work Works: A Status Report on Workplace Flexibility* (New York: Families and Work Institute, 2004), 22. Families and Work Institute found that 39 percent of employees surveyed thought that adopting flexible work arrangements could jeopardize their jobs. Respondents who were parents were even more likely to believe that "using flexible work options would have negative effects on their job advancement."

11. Catalyst, *Women and Men in U.S. Corporate Leadership: Same Workplace, Different Realities* (New York: Catalyst, 2004). In this study of senior executives, the majority said they did not use FWAs because of the potential career consequences.

12. Ibid.

13. Moen and Roehling, *The Career Mystique*, 186.

14. WFD Consulting, *The New Career Paradigm.*

15. Catalyst, *Women and Men in U.S. Corporate Leadership.*

16. National Academy of Sciences, *Beyond Bias and Barriers: Fulfilling the Potential of Women in Academic Science and Engineering* (Washington, DC: National Academies Press, 2006), 5–12.

17. Anna Bahney, "A Life Between Jobs," *New York Times*, June 8, 2006.

18. Ibid.

19. Families and Work Institute, *Generation & Gender in the Workplace* (New York: American Business Collaboration, 2004), 30.

20. Shapiro, Ingols, and Blake-Beard, "Optioning In Versus 'Opting Out'"; Catalyst, *Flexible Work Arrangements III: A Ten-Year Retrospective* (New York: Catalyst, 2000).

21. Elizabeth Dreike Almer and Steven E. Kaplan, "The Effects of Flexible Work Arrangements on Stressors, Burnout, and Behavioral Job Outcomes in Public Accounting," *Behavioral Research in Accounting* 14 (2002): 4. Almer and Kaplan state, "Typically professionals working under a flexible work arrangement negotiate their job content and expectations." See also Barney Olmsted, "Flexible Work Arrangements: From Accommodation to Strategy," *Employment Relations Today*, Summer 1995, 11. Olmsted says, "[D]uring the first decade and a half of their use, flexible work arrangements were considered by most managers to be employee-driven aberrations—ways to accommodate a few valued employees, while most people worked a standard, 40-hour, nine-to-five week."

22. Hans Morris, telephone interview by Anne Weisberg, tape recording, October 6, 2006.

23. Tuck School of Business at Dartmouth, "All Tuck's Women," *Tuck Today*, Spring 2006, http://www.tuck.dartmouth.edu/news/features/women.html. Elizabeth Rieke, senior director of brand strategy at Gap Inc., at Tuck's Women in Business conference in the fall of 2005, described the dilemma she is facing managing her work schedule and parental demands because Gap Inc. no longer allows "high-ranking" employees to work part-time.

24. James J. Sandman, telephone interview by Anne Weisberg and Jenna Carl, tape recording, September 25, 2006.

25. Sara A. Rogier and Margaret Y. Padgett, "The Impact of Utilizing a Flexible Work Schedule on the Perceived Career Advancement of Women," *Human Resource Development Quarterly* 15, no. 1 (2004): 99.

The authors constructed a hypothetical woman on an FWA and tracked her career progress. They found that "though the actual performance of this employee was identical in the two scheduling conditions, her job and career dedication and her advancement motivation were rated significantly lower in the flexible schedule condition than in the regular schedule condition." See also Michael K. Judiesch and Karen S. Lyness, "Left Behind? The Impact of Leaves of Absence on Managers' Career Success," *Academy of Management Journal* 42 (1999): 641–651. The authors found that those who took a leave of absence, regardless of the reason (including illness), had significantly fewer promotions and smaller salary increases. See also ch. 3, nn. 10–11.

26. Quotations from Sheilah Eisel and Kim B. Clark come from Lesley Stahl, "Staying at Home," *60 Minutes*, transcript of program segment, July 17, 2005.

27. Penelope J. E. Davies, Walter B. Denny, Frima Fox Hofrichter, Joseph Jacobs, Ann M. Roberts, and David L. Simon, *Janson's History of Art: The Western Tradition*, 7th ed. (Upper Saddle River, NJ: Pearson Education, 2007), 946–949. See also Francoise Gilot, *Matisse and Picasso: A Friendship in Art* (New York: Doubleday, 1990), 71–76; and Hilary Spurling, *Matisse the Master: A Life of Henri Matisse, The Conquest of Colour, 1909–1954* (New York: Alfred A. Knopf, 2005), 426–466.

Chapter 4

The quotation from Bill Strickland can be found in http://www.decaturdaily.com/decaturdaily/news/050916/center.shtml. Strickland, president and CEO of the Manchester Bidwell Corporation, is a social entrepreneur. He is a recipient of the MacArthur Foundation's Genius Grant and has been described as "the grandfather of the philanthropreneur movement." Knowledge@WPCarey, "Bill Strickland: Role Model for Social Entrepreneurship," January 3, 2007, http://knowledge.wpcarey.asu.edu/index.cfm?fa=viewfeature&id=1352.

1. Frank T. Piller, Kathrin Moeslein, and Christof M. Stotko, "Does Mass Customization Pay? An Economic Approach to Evaluate Customer Integration," *Production Planning & Control* 15, no. 4 (June 2004): 435–444.

2. Myra M. Hart, telephone interview by Anne Weisberg and Jenna Carl, tape recording, September 20, 2006.

3. Clayton M. Christensen, *The Innovator's Dilemma: When New Technologies Cause Great Firms to Fail* (Boston: Harvard Business School Press, 1997); Clayton M. Christensen and Michael E. Raynor, *The Innovator's Solution: Creating and Sustaining Successful Growth* (Boston: Harvard Business School Press, 2003); Richard Foster and Sara Kaplan, *Creative Destruction: Why Companies That Are Built to Last Underperform the Market—and How to Successfully Transform Them* (New York: Currency Doubleday, 2001).

4. For an introduction into social and psychological aspects of different stages in an adult's life, see Erik H. Erikson, *Identity and the Life Cycle* (New York: W. W. Norton, 1980).

5. Quotations from Shelly Lazarus in this book come from a telephone interview by Anne Weisberg and Cathleen Benko, tape recording, October 6, 2006.

6. Richard B. Freeman and Joel Rogers, *What Workers Want* (Ithaca, NY: Cornell University Press, 1999), 4–7.

7. Catalyst, *Two Careers, One Marriage: Making It Work in the Workplace* (New York: Catalyst, 1998).

8. Ibid.

9. Ruby Carlos, interview by Cathleen Benko, tape recording, Costa Mesa, CA, October 16, 2006.

10. National Academy of Sciences, *Beyond Bias and Barriers: Fulfilling the Potential of Women in Academic Science and Engineering* (Washington, DC: National Academies Press, 2006).

11. Kathy Gurchiek, "Study: Flexible Schedules Boost Performance, Productivity," Society for Human Resource Management Online, July 20, 2005, http://www.shrm.org/hrnews_published/archives/CMS_013419.asp.

12. Jyoti Thottam, "Reworking Work," *Time*, July 25, 2005.

13. Michelle Conlin, "Smashing the Clock," *BusinessWeek*, December 11, 2006.

14. Sylvia Ann Hewlett and Carolyn Buck Luce, "Extreme Jobs: The Dangerous Allure of the 70-Hour Workweek," *Harvard Business Review*, December 2006, 10.

Chapter 5

The quotation from Thomas W. Malone can be found in Thomas W. Malone, *The Future of Work: How the New Order of Business Will Shape*

Your Organization, Your Management Style and Your Life (Boston: Harvard Business School Press, 2004), ix.

1. "Deloitte" refers to one or more of Deloitte Touche Tohmatsu (a Swiss Verein, or association), its member firms, and their respective subsidiaries and affiliates. As a Swiss Verein, neither Deloitte Touche Tohmatsu nor any of its member firms has any liability for each other's acts or omissions. Each of the member firms is a separate and independent legal entity operating under "Deloitte," "Deloitte & Touche," "Deloitte Touche Tohmatsu," or other related names. Services are provided by the member firms or their subsidiaries or affiliates and not by the Deloitte Touche Tohmatsu Verein. Deloitte & Touche USA LLP is the U.S. member firm of Deloitte Touche Tohmatsu. In the United States, services are provided by the subsidiaries of Deloitte & Touche USA LLP (Deloitte & Touche LLP, Deloitte Consulting LLP, Deloitte Financial Advisory Services LLP, Deloitte Tax LLP, and their subsidiaries) and not by Deloitte & Touche USA LLP. [v.I.1]

2. Rich Karlgaard, "Digital Rules: Who Wants to Be Public?" Forbes.com, October 9, 2006, http://www.forbes.com/archive/forbes/2006/1009/031.html;jsessionid=abcUsKl55DLL0c2oLPu6q?token=MjkgT2N0 IDIwMDYgMTU6MTg6MTggKzAwMDA%3D.

3. Janet Wiscombe, "CEO Takes HR to Prime Time," *Workforce*, December 2002.

4. James Goodnight, "Ask James Goodnight: The Founder of SAS Explains How to Be Progressive on a Budget," *Inc.*, June 2006, http://www.inc.com/magazine/20060601/handson-ask-the-bigwig.html.

5. Kecia Serwin, telephone interview by Thomas C. Hayes and Jenna Carl, tape recording, October 26, 2006. All details and quotations in the following five paragraphs, except where otherwise noted, were provided by Kecia Serwin.

6. Jeff Chambers, telephone interview by Anne Weisberg, Thomas C. Hayes, and Jenna Carl, tape recording, September 13, 2006.

7. Jeff Chambers, transcript of panel discussion (from presentation at the Chief Human Resource Officer Executive Forum 2005, The Evolving Role of the CHRO in the 21st Century, New York, June 2005).

8. Arnold & Porter, "Arnold & Porter Named a 2006 Working Mother 100 Best Company by *Working Mother* Magazine," September 25, 2006, http://arnoldporter.com/news_news.cfm?publication_id=1368.

9. All quotations from James J. Sandman come from a telephone interview by Anne Weisberg and Jenna Carl, tape recording, September 25, 2006.

10. Quotations from Shelly Lazarus come from a telephone interview by Anne Weisberg and Cathleen Benko, tape recording, October 6, 2006.

11. Deloitte & Touche USA LLP, "Leadership: Meet Some of the People of Deloitte & Touche USA LLP," June 3, 2006, http://www.deloitte.com/dtt/leadership/0,1045,sid%253D2315.html.

12. Deloitte has won numerous awards, including BusinessWeek Online's 2006 list of "The Best Places to Launch a Career" (Deloitte was third on the list of fifty organizations); DiversityInc's 2005 list of "Top Companies in Diversity"; *LATINA Style*'s 2006 list of "50 Best Companies for Latinas"; *Working Mother*'s 2006 list of "Best Companies for Women of Color"; and *Working Mother*'s 2006 list of "100 Best Companies for Working Mothers" (2006 marks the thirteenth consecutive year that Deloitte has received this award).

13. Rosabeth Moss Kanter and Jane Roessner, "Deloitte & Touche (A): A Hole in the Pipeline," Case Study 9-300-012 (Boston: Harvard Business School, 1999).

14. Quotations from Douglas M. McCracken come from his article "Winning the Talent War for Women: Sometimes It Takes a Revolution," *Harvard Business Review*, November–December 2000.

15. Kanter and Roessner, "Deloitte & Touche (A)."

16. "Women Post Gains in Partnership Percentage: Percentage of Big Four Women Partners Tops 17%," *Public Accounting Report*, November 30, 2006, 4–7; "Clarification and Correction," *Public Accounting Report*, December 15, 2006, 3; and Deloitte & Touche USA LLP, The Initiative for the Retention and Advancement of Women, *2006 Annual Report* (New York: Deloitte Development LLC, 2007).

17. Deloitte & Touche USA LLP, The Initiative for the Retention and Advancement of Women, *2006 Annual Report.*

18. Deloitte & Touche USA LLP, The Initiative for the Retention and Advancement of Women, *2005 Annual Report* (New York: Deloitte Development LLC, 2006).

19. All quotations related to the 2006 Global People Commitment survey.

20. Corporate Voices for Working Families, *Business Impacts of Flexibility: An Imperative for Expansion* (Washington, DC: Corporate Voices for Working Families, 2005). Data is from a survey of forty-six partner organizations and in-depth interviews with a subgroup of fifteen self-selected partner organizations.

21. Barry Salzberg, e-mail conversation with Cathy Benko, April 4, 2007.

22. Cathy Gleason, interview by Cathleen Benko et al., tape recording, Foster City, CA, September 7, 2006.

23. Quotations from Beth Kelleher come from a telephone interview by Michelle Geromel, tape recording, October 23, 2006.

24. Quotations from Raj Jayashankar come from a telephone interview by Michelle Geromel, tape recording, October 23, 2006. The following story, one among many, illustrates how MCC is already happening in the sense that people are working out customized career paths over time, adjusting the four dimensions of MCC.

25. Rick Wackerbarth, telephone interview by Cathy Gleason, tape recording, August 28, 2006.

26. Jon Williams, telephone interview by Cathy Gleason, tape recording, August 23, 2006.

27. Quotations from Cathy Gleason come from an interview by Cathleen Benko et al., tape recording, Foster City, CA, September 7, 2006.

28. Jon Williams, telephone interview by Cathy Gleason, tape recording, August 23, 2006.

29. Ibid.

30. Joe Echevarria, Mass Career Customization Steering Committee, conference call, January 2, 2007.

31. Frank Piantidosi, telephone interview by Cathy Benko and Anne Weisberg, tape recording, February 1, 2007.

32. Owen Ryan, telephone interview by Cathy Benko and Anne Weisberg, tape recording, January 31, 2007.

33. Sharon Allen, conversation with Cathy Benko, New York, October 10, 2006.

Chapter 6

The quotation from Thomas A. Edison can be found in Claire Philpott, "Technology Transfer: Fuel for Oregon's Economic Engine," *Portland*

Business Journal, January 13, 2006, http://www.bizjournals.com/portland/
stories/2006/01/16/focus7.html?from_rss=1.

1. Bill Gates, *Business @ the Speed of Thought: Succeeding in the Digital Economy* (New York: Warner Books, 1999).

2. Richard Gondek, "Disaster Recovery: When More of the Same Isn't Better," *Journal of Business Strategy,* June 27, 2002. See also Barnaby J. Feder, "After the Attacks: The Recovery Experts," *New York Times,* September 17, 2001.

3. Dana G. Mead, *High Standards, Hard Choices: A CEO's Journey of Courage, Risk and Change* with Thomas C. Hayes (New York: Wiley, 2000).

4. Several publications have written about Deloitte's Personal Pursuits program. See, for example, Anne Fisher, "Happy Employees, Loyal Employees," *Fortune,* January 22, 2007; Tim O'Brien, "Why Do So Few Women Reach the Top of Big Law Firms?" *New York Times,* March 19, 2006; and Sue Shellenbarger, "Employers Step Up Efforts to Lure Stay-at-Home Mothers Back to Work," *Wall Street Journal,* February 9, 2006.

Chapter 7

The quotation from Cynthia Ozick can be found in Cynthia Ozick, "The Shock of Teapots," *Metaphor & Memory* (New York: Vintage Press, 1991), 144.

1. Lyn Jeffery, telephone interview by Anne Weisberg, Thomas C. Hayes, and Jenna Carl, tape recording, November 9, 2006.

2. Edward E. Lawler III and Christopher G. Worley, *Built to Change: How to Achieve Sustained Organizational Effectiveness* (San Francisco: Jossey-Bass, 2006), xv.

3. Ibid., 231.

4. Ibid.

5. Frank Rose, "Commercial Break," *Wired,* December 2006, http://www.wired.com/wired/archive/14.12/tahoe_pr.html.

6. Gartner, "Gartner Highlights Seven Core Benefits of Web 2.0 for Traditional Industries," December 4, 2006, http://www.gartner.com/it/page.jsp?id=499154.

7. "Highlights and Predictions: Farewell to Bill Gates; Hello to Second Life," *Financial Times,* December 4, 2006. Geoff Nairn predicts that Cisco's TelePresence video system will allow people to "wave goodbye to unnecessary business trips."

8. "Cisco Connected Real Estate (CCRE) and Environmental Sustainability: An Overview for Business Decision Makers," Cisco presentation (Cisco Systems, 2006). E-mailed to Cathleen Benko from Christina S. Kite, December 8, 2006.

9. Christine S. Kite, telephone interview by Cathleen Benko, Anne Weisberg, and Thomas C. Hayes, November 27, 2006.

10. "Highlights and Predictions," *Financial Times*.

11. Leslie A. Perlow, "Why Is a Job a Job?" unpublished working paper, Harvard Business School, Boston, 2006.

12. Ibid.

13. Citigroup, "Corporate Citizenship," http://www.citigroup.com/citigroup/citizen/diversity/index.htm.

14. Information and quotations from Ana Duarte-McCarthy come from a telephone interview by Anne Weisberg and Thomas C. Hayes, tape recording, November 15, 2006.

15. "Work-Life Balance: Life Beyond Pay," *Economist*, June 15, 2006.

16. Quotations from Lyn Jeffery come from a telephone interview by Anne Weisberg, Thomas C. Hayes, and Jenna Carl, tape recording, November 9, 2006.

17. "Wikipedia: About," http://en.wikipedia.org/wiki/Wikipedia:About.

18. Eric Auchard, "LinkedIn Adds Yellow-Pages-Like Services Directory," Reuters.com, October 16, 2006, http://today.reuters.com/news/articlenews.aspx?type=internetNews&storyid=2006-10-16T095153Z_01_N15353899_RTRUKOC_0_US-MEDIA-LINKEDIN.xml&src=rss.; Michael V. Copeland, "The Missing Link," *Business 2.0*, December 2006, 118–124.

19. Ken Dychtwald, Robert Morison, and Tamara J. Erickson, *Workforce Crisis: How to Beat the Coming Shortage of Skills and Talent* (Boston: Harvard Business School Press, 2006).

20. For examples of formal reentry support programs initiated by large knowledge-service organizations, see Sue Shellenbarger, "Employers Step Up Efforts to Lure Stay-at-Home Mothers Back to Work," *Wall Street Journal*, February 9, 2006; and accountingweb.com, "Re-entry Programs Target Professional Women," May 16, 2006, http://www.accountingweb.com/cgi-bin/item.cgi?id=102156&d=815&h=817&f=816&da.

21. Edward E. Lawler III, transcript of panel discussion (from presentation at the Chief Human Resource Officer Executive Forum 2005,

The Evolving Role of the CHRO in the 21st Century, New York, June 2005).

22. Leigh Buchanan, "The Young and the Restful," *Harvard Business Review*, November 2004.

23. Adrian Wooldridge, "The Battle for Brainpower," *Economist*, October 5, 2006, http://www.economist.com/surveys/displaystory.cfm ?story_id=E1_SJGTRJQ.

24. Ibid.

25. Alicia H. Munnell and Amy Chasse, "Working Longer: A Potential Win-Win Proposition" (paper presented at Work Options for Mature Americans conference, University of Notre Dame, Notre Dame, IN, December 8, 2003).

26. Ben S. Bernanke, "The Coming Demographic Transition: Will We Treat Future Generations Fairly?" (speech to the Economic Club of Washington, Washington, DC, October 4, 2006).

27. Phil Strause, conversation with Cathleen Benko, December 8, 2006.

BIBLIOGRAPHY

Sources Cited in This Book

"All Tuck's Women." *Tuck Today*, Spring 2006, October 18, 2006. http://www.tuck.dartmouth.edu/news/features/women.html (accessed October 18, 2006).

Almer, Elizabeth Dreike, and Steven E. Kaplan. "The Effects of Flexible Work Arrangements on Stressors, Burnout, and Behavioral Job Outcomes in Public Accounting." *Behavioral Research in Accounting* 14 (2002).

Alsop, Ronald. "Ph.D. Shortage: Business Schools Seek Professors." *Wall Street Journal*, January 9, 2007.

American Institute of Certified Public Accountants (AICPA) Work/Life & Women's Initiatives Executive Committee. *AICPA Work/Life and Women's Initiatives 2004 Research.* New York: AICPA, 2004.

"Arnold & Porter Named a 2006 Working Mother 100 Best Company by Working Mother Magazine." Press release, September 25, 2006. http://arnoldporter.com/news_news.cfm?publication_id=1368 (accessed November 6, 2006).

Auchard, Eric. "LinkedIn Adds Yellow-Pages-Like Services Directory." Reuters, October 16, 2006. http://today.reuters.com/news/article news.aspx?type=internetNews&storyid=2006-10-16T095153Z_01 _N15353899_RTRUKOC_0_US-MEDIA-LINKEDIN.xml&src=rss (accessed November 24, 2006).

Bahney, Anna. "A Life Between Jobs." *New York Times*, June 8, 2006.

Barboza, David. "Sharp Labor Shortage in China May Lead to World Trade Shift." *New York Times*, April 3, 2006.

Belkin, Lisa. "Life's Work; Flex Time for the Rest of Us." *New York Times*, December 17, 2006.

Benko, Cathleen, and F. Warren McFarlan. *Connecting the Dots: Aligning Projects with Objectives in Unpredictable Times*. Boston: Harvard Business School Press, 2003.

Bernanke, Ben S. "The Coming Demographic Transition: Will We Treat Future Generations Fairly?" Speech to the Economic Club of Washington. Washington, DC, October 4, 2006.

Bianchi, Suzanne, John P. Robinson, and Melissa A. Milkie. *Changing Rhythms of American Family Life*. New York: American Sociological Association and Russell Sage Foundation, 2006.

Britz, Jennifer Delahunty. "To All the Girls I've Rejected." *New York Times*, March 23, 2006.

Buchanan, Leigh. "The Young and the Restful." *Harvard Business Review*, November 2004.

Catalyst. *Flexible Work Arrangements III: A Ten-Year Retrospective*. New York: Catalyst. 2000.

———. *The Next Generation: Today's Professionals, Tomorrow's Leaders*. New York: Catalyst, 2001.

———. *Two Careers, One Marriage: Making It Work in the Workplace*. New York: Catalyst, 1998.

———. *Women and Men in U.S. Corporate Leadership: Same Workplace, Different Realities*. New York: Catalyst, 2004.

———. *Women in Law: Making the Case*. New York: Catalyst, 2001.

Catalyst, Center for Education of Women at the University of Michigan, and University of Michigan Business School. *Women and the MBA: Gateway to Opportunity*. New York: Catalyst, 2000.

Catalyst, Families and Work Institute, and the Center for Work & Family at Boston College. *Leaders in a Global Economy: A Study of Executive Women and Men*. New York: Catalyst, 2002.

"CEO Takes HR to Prime Time—Between the Lines—Jim Goodnight, SAS." *Workforce*, December 2002.

Chambers, Jeff. Transcript of panel discussion from presentation at the Chief Human Resource Officer Executive Forum 2005, The Evolving Role of the CHRO in the 21st Century, New York, June 2005.

Christensen, Clayton M. *The Innovator's Dilemma: When New Technologies Cause Great Firms to Fail.* Boston: Harvard Business School Press, 1997.

Christensen Clayton M., and Michael E. Raynor. *The Innovator's Solution: Creating and Sustaining Successful Growth.* Boston: Harvard Business School Press, 2003.

"Cisco Connected Real Estate (CCRE) and Environmental Sustainability: An Overview for Business Decision Makers." Cisco presentation, 2006.

Citigroup.com. "Diversity" description, October 2006. http://www.citigroup.com/citigroup/citizen/diversity/index.htm (accessed November 23, 2006).

Cohen, Robin, and Linda Kornfeld. "Women Leaders Boost Profit." *Barron's Online,* September 4, 2006. http://online.barrons.com/article_search/SB115715054502452224.html?mod=search&KEYWORDS=kornfeld&COLLECTION=barrons/archive (accessed September 6, 2006).

The Conference Board, Inc., the Partnership for 21st Century Skills, Corporate Voices for Working Families, and the Society for Human Resource Management. *Are They Really Ready to Work? Employers' Perspectives on the Basic Knowledge and Applied Skills of New Entrants to the 21st Century U.S. Workforce.* Alexandria. VA: Society for Human Resource Management. 2006.

Conlin, Michelle. "Smashing the Clock." *BusinessWeek,* December 11, 2006.

Copeland, Michael V. "The Missing Link." *Business 2.0,* December 2006.

Corporate Voices for Working Families. *Business Impacts of Flexibility: An Imperative for Expansion.* Washington, DC: Corporate Voices for Working Families, 2005.

Daly, Kerry, and Linda Hawkins. "Fathers and the Work-family Politic." *Ivey Business Journal* (July–August 2005).

Deloitte & Touche USA LLP. "Facts & Figures." Deloitte.com, June 3, 2006. http://www.deloitte.com/dtt/leadership/0.1045.sid%253D2282.00.html (accessed November 20, 2006).

———. *Flexible Work Arrangement Turnover Study.* New York: Deloitte & Touche USA LLP, April 2004.

———. The Initiative for the Retention and Advancement of Women. *2005 Annual Report.* New York: Deloitte Development LLC 2005.

Deloitte Research. "It's 2008: Do You Know Where Your Talent Is?" New York: Deloitte Development LLC, 2004.

Dunnewind, Stephanie. "Attitudes About Paternity Leave Are Changing." *Seattle Times*, November 19, 2003.

Dychtwald, Ken D., Robert Morison, and Tamara Erickson. *Workforce Crisis: How to Beat the Coming Shortage of Skills and Talent*. Boston: Harvard Business School Press, 2006.

Eisner, Susan. "Managing Generation Y." *SAM Advanced Management Journal* 70, no. 4 (2005).

Elias, Marilyn. "The Family-First Generation." *USA Today*, December 12, 2004.

Erikson, Erik H. *Identity and the Life Cycle*. New York: W.W. Norton & Company Inc., 1980.

Evans, Carol. *This Is How We Do It: The Working Mother's Manifesto*. New York: Hudson Street Press and Working Mother Media, 2006.

Families and Work Institute. *Generation & Gender in the Workplace*. New York: American Business Collaboration, 2004.

———. *When Work Works: A Status Report on Workplace Flexibility*. New York: Families and Work Institute, 2004.

Farrell, Diana, and Andrew J. Grant. "China's Looming Talent Shortage." *McKinsey Quarterly*, no. 4 (2005): 70–79.

Feder, Barnaby J. "After the Attacks: The Recovery Experts." *New York Times*, September 17, 2001.

Fisher, Anne. "Happy Employees, Loyal Employees." *Fortune*, January 22, 2007.

———. "Have You Outgrown Your Job?" *Fortune*, August 21, 2006.

"For Many, Their Cell Phone Has Become Their Only Phone." *USA Today*. March 24, 2003. http://www.usatoday.com/tech/news/2003 -03-24-cell-phones_x.htm (accessed October 11, 2006).

Foster, Richard, and Sara Kaplan. *Creative Destruction: Why Companies That Are Built to Last Underperform the Market—and How to Successfully Transform Them*. New York: Currency Doubleday, 2001.

Freeman, Richard B., and Joel Rogers. *What Workers Want*. Ithaca. NY: Cornell University Press, 1999.

Galinsky, Ellen. "When Work Works." Paper presented at Corporate Voices for Working Families Annual Meeting, Washington, DC, June 2006.

Gartner.com. "Gartner Highlights Seven Core Benefits of Web 2.0 for Traditional Industries." Press release, December 4, 2006. http://www .gartner.com/it/page.jsp?id=499154 (accessed 23 January 2007).

Gates, Bill. *Business @ the Speed of Thought: Succeeding in the Digital Economy*. New York: Warner Books, Inc., 1999.

Gerdes, Lindsey. "The Best Places to Launch a Career: The Top 50 Employers for New College Grads." *BusinessWeek*, September 18, 2006.

Goldin, Claudia. "The Quiet Revolution That Transformed Women's Employment. Education. and Family." Paper presented at the Richard T. Ely Lecture. Harvard University, Cambridge, MA, January 6, 2006.

Gondek, Richard. "Disaster Recovery: When More of the Same Isn't Better." *Journal of Business Strategy*, June 27, 2002.

Goodnight, James. "Ask James Goodnight: The Founder of SAS Explains How to be Progressive on a Budget." *Inc.*, June 2006. http://www.inc.com/magazine/20060601/handson-ask-the-bigwig.html (accessed November 6, 2006).

Grossman, Robert J. "The Truth About the Coming Labor Shortage." *HR Magazine*, March 2005.

Gurchiek, Kathy. "Study: Flexible schedules boost performance, productivity," Society for Human Resource Management Online, HR News Page. 20 July 2005. http://www.shrm.org/hrnews_published/archives/CMS_013419.asp (accessed February 8, 2007).

Hart, Myra M. "Models of Success." Paper presented at Models of Success Initiative Breakfast at Harvard Business School, Cambridge, MA, May 9, 2006).

Hewlett, Sylvia Ann. *Off-ramps and On-ramps: Keeping Talented Women on the Road to Success.* Boston: Harvard Business School Press, 2007.

Hewlett, Sylvia Ann, and Carolyn Buck Luce. "Extreme Jobs: The Dangerous Allure of the 70-Hour Workweek." *Harvard Business Review*, December 2006.

"Highlights and Predictions: Farewell to Bill Gates; Hello to Second Life." *Financial Times*, December 4, 2006.

Holland, Kelley. "When Work Time Isn't Face Time." *New York Times*, December 3, 2006.

Jackson, Maggie. "Finding the Work-Life Balance." *Boston Globe*, June 19, 2005.

Judiesch, Michael K., and Karen S. Lyness. "Left Behind? The Impact of Leaves of Absence on Managers' Career Success." *Academy of Management Journal* 42 (1999.

Kanter, Rosabeth Moss, and Jane Roessner. "Deloitte & Touche (A): A Hole in the Pipeline." Case Study No. 9-300-012. Boston: Harvard Business School Press, 1999.

Karlgaard, Rich. "Digital Rules: Who Wants to Be Public?" *Forbes.com*, October 9, 2006. http://www.forbes.com/archive/forbes/2006/1009/

031.html;jsessionid=abcUsKl55DLL0c2oLPu6q?token=MjkgT2N0IDI
wMDYgMTU6MTg6MTggKzAwMDA%3D (accessed October 27,
2006).

King, Jacqueline. *Gender Equity in Higher Education: 2006.* Washington,
DC: American Council on Education, 2006.

Knight, Rebecca. "Entrants to U.S. Workforce Ill-Prepared." *Financial
Times,* October 1, 2006.

Lawler, Edward E. III. Panel discussion at the Chief Human Resource
Officer Executive Forum 2005, "The Evolving Role of the CHRO in
the 21st Century." New York, June 2005.

Lawler, Edward E. III, and Christopher G. Worley. *Built to Change: How to
Achieve Sustained Organizational Effectiveness.* San Francisco: Jossey-
Bass, 2006.

Levine, James A., and Todd L. Pittinsky. *Working Fathers: New Strategies
for Balancing Work and Family.* Fort Washington, PA: Harvest Books,
1997.

Lewin, Tamar. "At Colleges: Women Are Leaving Men in the Dust." *New
York Times,* July 9, 2006.

Lovgren, Stefan. "Can Cell-Phone Recycling Help African Gorillas?" January 20, 2006. http://news.nationalgeographic.com/news/2006/01/
0120_060120_cellphones.html (accessed October 11, 2006).

Malone, Thomas W. Interview by Howard Dresner. March 8, 2005.
http://www.gartner.com/research/fellows/asset_126360_1176.jsp (accessed October 6, 2006).

"Manpower: The World of Work." *The Economist,* January 4, 2007.

Mattis, Mary. "New Forms of Flexible Work Arrangements for Managers
and Professionals." *Human Resource Planning* 13, no. 2 (1990).

McCracken, Douglas M. "Winning the Talent War for Women: Sometimes It Takes a Revolution." *Harvard Business Review,* November–
December 2000.

McGrath, Monica, Marla Driscoll, and Mary Gross. *Back in the Game:
Returning to Business After a Hiatus.* Philadelphia, PA, and Austin,
TX: Wharton Center for Leadership and Change and The Forté
Foundation, 2005.

Mead, Dana G., with Thomas C. Hayes. *High Standards, Hard Choices, A
CEO's Journey of Courage, Risk and Change.* New York: John Wiley &
Sons, Inc., 2000.

Miller, Jody. "Get a Life!" *Fortune,* November 28, 2005.

Moen, Phyllis, and Patricia Roehling. *The Career Mystique: Cracks in the American Dream.* Lanham, MD: Rowman & Littlefield Publishers Inc., 2004.

Moen, Phyllis, and Stephen Sweet. "From 'Work-Family' to 'Flexible Careers'? A Life Course Reframing." *Community, Work & Family* 7, no. 2 (2004).

Munnell, Alicia H., and Amy Chasse. "Working Longer: A Potential Win-Win Proposition." Paper presented at "Work Options for Mature Americans," University of Notre Dame, Notre Dame, Indiana, December 8, 2003.

National Academy of Sciences. *Beyond Bias and Barriers: Fulfilling the Potential of Women in Academic Science and Engineering.* Washington, DC: National Academies Press, 2006.

National Association of Law Placement. Press release, December 7, 2006. http://www.nalp.org/press/details.php?id=65 (accessed 22 January 2007).

O'Brien, Tim. "Why Do So Few Women Reach the Top of Big Law Firms?" *New York Times,* March 19, 2006.

Olmsted, Barney. "Flexible Work Arrangements: From Accommodation to Strategy." *Employment Relations Today,* Summer 1995.

Orrange, Robert. "Aspiring Law and Business Professionals' Orientations to Work and Family Life." *Journal of Family Issues* 23, no. 2 (2002): 287–317.

Perlow, Leslie A. "Why Is a Job a Job?" Working paper. Harvard Business School, Boston, MA, 2006.

Perry, Joellen. "Exodus of Skilled Workers Leaves Germany in a Bind." *Wall Street Journal,* January 3, 2007.

Piller, Frank T., Kathrin Moeslein, and Christof M. Stotko. "Does Mass Customization Pay? An Economic Approach to Evaluate Customer Integration." *Production Planning & Control* 15, no. 4 (June 2004): 435–444.

"Re-entry Programs Target Professional Women." accountingweb.com, May 16, 2006. http://www.accountingweb.com/cgi-bin/item.cgi?id=102156&d=815&h=817&f=816&da (accessed November 29, 2006).

Richert, Eric, and David Rush. "How New Infrastructure Provided Flexibility, Controlled Cost and Empowered Workers at Sun Microsystems." *Journal of Corporate Real Estate* 7, no. 3 (2005): 271–279.

Ripley, Amanda. "Who Says a Woman Can't Be Einstein?" *Time*, March 7, 2005.

Roberts, Sam. "51% of Women Are Now Living Without Spouse." *New York Times*, January 16, 2007.

Rodgers, Charles. "The Flexible Workplace: What Have We Learned?" *Human Resource Management* 31, no. 3 (1992): 183–199.

Rogier, Sara A., and Margaret Y. Padgett. "The Impact of Utilizing a Flexible Work Schedule on the Perceived Career Advancement of Women." *Human Resource Development Quarterly* 15, no. 1 (2004).

Rose, Frank. "Commercial Break." *Wired.com*, http://www.wired.com/wired/archive/14.12/tahoe_pr.html (accessed January 23, 2007).

Rulison, Larry. "Gen Y in Search of Flexibility." *Philadelphia Business Journal*, September 22, 2003.

Sacks, Danielle. "Scenes from the Culture Clash." *Fast Company*, January 2006.

Schwartz, Felice N. "Management Women and the New Facts of Life." *Harvard Business Review*, January–February 1989.

"The Search for Talent: Why It's Getting Harder to Find." *The Economist*, October 7, 2006.

Shapiro, Mary, Cynthia Ingols, and Stacy Blake-Beard. "Optioning In' Versus 'Opting Out': Women Using Flexible Work Arrangements for Career Success." *CGO Insights*, January 2007.

Shellenbarger, Sue. "Employers Step Up Efforts to Lure Stay at Home Mothers Back to Work." *Wall Street Journal*, February 9, 2006.

Society for Human Resource Management. *SHRM 2003 Eldercare Survey*. Alexandria, VA: SHRM Research, 2003.

"Staying at Home" with Lesley Stahl. CBS News. *60 Minutes*, July 17, 2005.

Thottam, Jyoti. "Reworking Work." *Time*, July 25, 2005.

Tivo.com, "What Is TiVo?," February 14, 2007, http://www.tivo.com/1.0.asp (accessed February 14, 2007).

Tse, Edward. "China's Five Surprises." *Strategy + Business*, January 16, 2006.

Tucci, Linda. "Gartner: Firms at Risk of Losing Women Technologists." SearchCIO.com., December 5, 2006. http://searchcio.techtarget.com/originalContent/0.289142.sid19_gci1233089.00.html?track=NL-162&ad=574445 (accessed January 24, 2007).

U.S. Bureau of Labor Statistics. *Women in the Labor Force: A Databook*. Washington, DC: GPO, 2005.

————. *America's Families and Living Arrangements: 2003*. Washington, DC: GPO, 2004.

U.S. Census Bureau. "Maternity Leave and Employment Patterns of First-Time Mothers. 1961–2000." Current Population Reports. Washington, DC: GPO, 2005.

U.S. Department of Education, National Center for Education Statistics. "Table 246. Degrees conferred by degree-granting institutions. by level of degree and sex of student: Selected years, 1869-70 through 2013-14." Digest of Education Statistics 2005 Page. June 2006. http://nces.ed.gov/programs/digest/d05/tables/dt05 246.asp (accessed January 31, 2007).

U.S. Department of Labor. "Women in the Labor Force in 2005." Women's Bureau Page. June 19, 2006. www.dol.gov/wb/factsheets/Qf-laborforce-.05.htm (accessed May 20, 2006).

WebSiteOptimization.com. "China to Pass U.S. in Total Broadband Lines." October 2006. WebSiteOptimization.com/bw/ (accessed November 28, 2006).

WFD Consulting. *The New Career Paradigm: Attracting and Retaining Critical Talent*. Newton, MA: American Business Collaboration, 2006.

Wikipedia.com. "Henri Matisse Biography." http://en.wikipedia.org/wiki/Matisse.

————. "Wikipedia: The Free Encyclopedia."

Williams, Joan, and Cynthia Thomas Calvert. *Solving the Part-Time Puzzle: The Law Firm's Guide to Balanced Hours*. Washington, DC: National Association of Law Placement, 2004.

Wooldridge, Adrian. "The Battle for Brainpower." *Economist.com*, October 5, 2006. http://www.economist.com/surveys/displaystory.cfm?story_id=E1_SJGTRJQ (accessed October 5, 2006).

"Work-Life Balance: Life Beyond Pay." *The Economist*, June 15, 2006.

Additional Sources

Ashkenas, Ron, Dave Ulrich, Todd Jick, and Steve Kerr. *The Boundaryless Organization: Breaking the Chains of Organizational Structure*. San Francisco: Jossey-Bass Publishers, 1995.

Arthur, Michael, and Rousseau, Denise, eds. *The Boundaryless Career: A New Employment Principle for a New Organizational Era*. New York: Oxford University Press, 1996.

Blumenthal, Ralph. "Unfilled City Manager Positions Hint at Future Government Gap." *New York Times*, January 11, 2007.

Davenport, Thomas H. *Thinking for a Living: How to Get Better Performances and Results from Knowledge Workers.* Boston: Harvard Business School Press, 2005.

Fels, Anna. *Necessary Dreams.* New York: Anchor Books, 2004.

Malone, Thomas W. *The Future of Work: How the New Order of Business Will Shape Your Organization, Your Management Style, and Your Life.* Boston: Harvard Business School Press, 2004.

Maneiro, Lisa, and Sherry Sullivan. *The Opt-Out Revolt: Why People Are Leaving Companies to Create Kaleidoscope Careers.* Mountain View, CA: Davies-Black Publishing, 2006.

Naisbitt, John, and Patricia Aburdene. *Megatrends 2000: Ten New Directions for the 1990's.* New York: William Morrow and Company, Inc., 1990.

Nash, Laura, and Howard Stevenson. *Just Enough: Tools for Creating Success in Your Work and Life.* Hoboken, NJ: John Wiley & Sons, 2004.

Osterman, Paul, ed. *Broken Ladders: Managerial Careers in the New Economy.* New York: Oxford University Press, 1996.

Perlow, Leslie A. *Finding Time: How Corporations, Individuals and Families Can Benefit from New Work Practices.* Ithaca, NY: ILR Press, 1997.

Rapaport, Rhona, and Lotte Bailyn. *Relinking Life and Work: Toward a Better Future.* New York: Ford Foundation, 1996.

Rousseau, Denise. "The Idiosyncratic Deal: Flexibility versus Fairness?" *Organizational Dynamics*, Vol. 29, No. 4. Burlington, MA: Elsevier Science, Inc., 2001.

"Women and the World Economy: A Guide to Womenomics." *The Economist*, April 15, 2006.

INDEX

accounting profession, 61–62

adaptive organizations, 170

Allen, Sharon, 144–145

American Express, 95

American Institute of Certified Public Accountants, 61–62

American workforce. *See* workforce

anticipatory career anxiety, 43

Arnold & Porter, 7, 72, 115–117

Association of Executive Search Consultants, 45

baby boomers, 5, 185

Bernanke, Ben S., 185

Best Buy, 94

Beyond Bias and Barriers (National Academy of Sciences), 65–66

biological clocks, 43

birth rates, 29

bottom-up value creation, 180–181, 182

brain drain risk, 152

broadband connectivity, 51

Built to Change (Lawler and Worley), 170

built-to-change (b2change) organizations, 170

business case, for MCC adoption, 78, 150–156

business metrics, 186

Business Opportunities for Leadership Diversity project, 93

career continuum, 59–61

career conversations, 137–140, 161–162, 170–171

career dimensions, 90–97

changes in, over time, 83–85

customization of, 157–158

interdependence among, 95–97

Location/Schedule, 93–94, 96, 97

in MCC profile, 15–16, 84

movement along, 158–159

Pace, 91–92, 96, 97

career dimensions *(continued)*
  Role, 94–95, 96, 97
  Workload, 92–93, 96, 97, 141
career-life fit, 113, 117, 124, 125,
    126, 136. *See also* work-life
    balance
  flexible work arrangements
    and, 11–14
Career Mystique (Moen and
    Roehling), 32, 40, 63–64
career options
  characteristics of customized, 35
  MCC and, 22–23, 82, 86–87
  transparency of, 86–87, 90, 170,
    180
  for women, 39–44
career penalties, 62–64
career planning, 99–100, 135–142
career progression
  ladder model of, 3–5, 82, 88
  lattice model of, 3–5, 77–78,
    168–169
Catalyst, 39
cellular phones, 52
Chambers, Jeff, 115
change, adapting to, 167–168
change leadership, 170
change management, 85
children
  effect of, on women's career
    paths, 39–44
  fathers and, 45–46
China, 29, 31
Chubb Group, 93
chunking, 179
Cisco Systems, 172–177, 181
Citigroup, 42–43, 68, 177–179
Clark, Kim B., 75

clients, long-term relationships
    with, 111, 117, 145
collaboration, 82, 159
college graduates
  shortage of, 27
  women as majority of, 37
commitment, questioned, of FWA
    employees, 73
communication, between man-
    agers and employees, 100,
    137–140, 161–162, 170–171
communications technology,
    impact of, 6, 51–55, 153–154
competitive advantage, of MCC,
    3, 9, 143–144, 147
continuity of service, 111, 117,
    145
Cook, Michael, 121
corporate ladder
  versus corporate lattice, 3–5, 88
  drawbacks of, 82
corporate lattice. *See also*
    lattice-type organizations
  advantages of, 9
  case for, 77–78, 168–169
  introduction to, 3–5
  value creation in, 180–181
coworkers, resentment of, over
    FWAs, 72
credibility, 169
criterions, 100–101, 135, 163
customer loyalty, 111, 117

Daly, Kerry, 47
Deloitte, 120–144
  career customization at,
    127–145

FWAs at, 123–127
journey toward MCC by,
    120–124
leadership at, 142–144
MCC pilots 128–144
Personal Pursuits program,
    158–159
Women's Initiative program,
    122–123, 124
demographics, changing, 29–30
Denholm, Robyn, 54–55
dial-down, MCC dimensions, 20,
    66, 100, 102, 130, 133, 172
dial-up, MCC dimensions, 20, 83,
    102, 133, 137, 172
dimensions. *See* career dimensions
diversity, 185–186
dual-career households, 33–34,
    187–188
dual-income households, 2
Duarte-McCarthy, Ana, 178, 179,
    180
Dychtwald, Ken, 29

Echevarria, Joe, 143
Ecology of Careers study, 61
Eisel, Sheilah, 74–75, 96
elder-care responsibilities, 35–36
e-mail, 51
employee-employer relationship,
    8, 89–90, 100, 106–107, 159
employee loyalty, 21–23, 90, 111,
    117, 145, 178, 183–184
employee output, as measurement
    criterion, 54
employee profiles. *See* MCC
    profiles

employee retention
    flexibility options and, 88–90
    FWAs and, 135
    MCC and, 21–23, 82, 106,
        134–135, 183–184
employees, empowering, 88–90
employee turnover rate, 62
    analysis of, 152–153
    gender gap in, 121–122
enablement, 159–160
enterprise value map (EVM)
    approach, 150–153
entitlement misconceptions,
    159–160
equalizer, 83, 85

face time, 54, 94
fairness, 87
Families and Work Institute,
    47–49, 62–63, 66–67
family priorities. *See also* career-
    life fit
    of Generations X and Y, 48–51
family structures, changes in, 6,
    31–36
fathers, caregiving responsibilities
    of, 34, 45–46, 65–66
Federal Reserve Board, 185
flexible work arrangements
    (FWAs)
    career continuum and, 59–61
    case study, 74–75
    comparison between MCC and,
        87–88, 160–161
    costs of, 69–70
    coworker resentment and, 72
    at Deloitte, 123–127

flexible work arrangements
  (FWAs) (continued)
  desired by men, 47–48
  definition of, 11, 13
  employee retention and, 135
  entitlement status and, 70
  feelings of inadequacy and,
    72–73
  lack of fit between job and, 69
  lack of scalability of, 67–68
  versus MCCs, 160–161
  men, and 47–48, 64–66
  overhead for, 69–70
  performance evaluations and,
    70–71
  questions of commitment and,
    73
  reasons for, 68
  rejection of, by men, 64–67
  at senior levels, 68–69
  shortcomings of, 11–14, 57–76
  stigma attached to, 62–66, 73, 131
  trade-offs of, 71–72
  typical options for, 58–59
  utilization rates for, 46, 62
fluidity, 85
Fortune 500 companies, turnover
  rate in, 62
Fortune Magazine, 44–45
Frost, Robert, 165

Galinsky, Ellen, 46–47
Gap Inc., 68–69
Gates, Bill, 31, 147
gender diversity, 185–186
General Electric, 158

Generation X
  expectations of, 6, 7, 20, 48–51
  leaving corporate ladder, 66
Generation Y
  expectations of, 6, 7, 48–51
  fathers, 46, 48–49
  men, 68
  social networking by, 177, 180
Gleason, Cathy, 128, 136,
    139–140, 143
global workforce
goal setting, 98–102, 137–138,
    170–171
Goodnight, James, 111, 112–113

Hart, Myra M., 10, 82
Harvard Business School, 39, 75,
    176–177
Hawkins, Linda, 47
household profiles, diversity in, 32

immigration rates, 5–6, 29, 31
India, 29, 31
information technology, impact
  of, 6, 51–55, 153–154
instant messaging, 51–52
Internet, 167–168

Jayashankar, Raj, 131, 133
Jeffery, Lyn, 180, 182
JetBlue Airways, 52
job changing, 66–67
job mobility, 51
job modularity, 176–177

job satisfaction, 88–90
Johnson & Johnson, 93

Kelleher, Beth, 131, 133
Keller, Jesse, 66
knowledge-driven economy, 2
knowledge workers
  job searches by, 182–183
  shortage of skilled, 27–31

labor force. *See* workforce
ladder model. *See* corporate
  ladder
lateral movement, 158
lattice model. *See* corporate
  lattice
lattice-type organizations,
  109–110
  Arnold & Porter, 115–117
  Citigroup, 177–179
  Deloitte, 120–144
  MCC framework for, 169–171
  Ogilvy & Mather, 118–120
  option value of, 88–90
  retention in, 183–184
  SAS, 110–115
  Sun Microsystems, 53–55
law firms, 62, 92
Lawler, Edward E., L., 170
Lazarus, Shelly, 53, 87, 118
leadership, 120, 170
  diversity in, 185–86
  talent, 184–85
lifestyles, changing, 31–36
LinkedIn, 181

Location/Schedule dimension,
  93–94, 96, 97
Lockheed Martin, 21–22

Malone, Thomas W., 52
management jobs, women in, 5
managers
  buy-in from, 154–55
  communication between
    employees and, 100, 137–140,
    161–162, 170–171
  MCC profiles of, 155–56
  MCC pilots, 127–145
  partnership between employees
    and, 89–90, 161–162
marriage, division of labor in,
  187–188
marriage rate, decrease in, 33
mass career customization
  (MCC). *See also* MCC
  profiles
  adaptability of, 157
  applicability of, 86
  benefits of, 14, 80–82, 105–107,
    169–171, 181–182
  business case for, 78, 150–156
  career dimensions of, 15–16,
    85–86, 90–97, 157–159
  career example, 17–20
  challenges of, 156–165
  comparison between FWAs
    and, 87–88, 160–161
  core characteristics of, 82–88
  at Deloitte, 127–45
  eligibility criteria for, 100–101,
    135, 163

mass career customization
  (MCC) *(continued)*
 as emerging standard, 8–11
 employee retention and, 21–23,
  82, 106, 134–135, 183–184
 fluidity of, 85
 framework, 90–97
 improved efficiency and,
  153–154
 informal, 17–20, 171, 179
 integrating into existing systems,
  98–102, 134–142, 162–163
 introduction to, 2–3, 14–17
 lattice model and, 3–5, 77–79
 leadership pipeline and, 184–185
 measuring success of, 164–165
 multidimensional nature of,
  85–86
 naming of, 79
 option value of, 22–23, 88–90,
  171
 pilots (*see* MCC pilots)
 possibilities of, 148–150
 principles of, 8
 promotion of diversity and,
  185–186
 recruitment and, 21–23, 182–183
 trade-offs, managing 20–22
 transparency of, 85, 86–87, 90,
  170, 180
mass product customization
  (MPC), 3, 79–81, 106–107
maternity leave, 11
Matisse, Henri, 57, 76
MCC. *See* mass career
  customization
MCC profiles
 adjustments to, 83–85

 case study, 113–114
 creating own, 171–172
 evolution of, 101–105
 initial, 100–101
 for managers, 155–156
 options provided by, 15–16
 standard, 84, 91, 171
 template, 173
McCracken, Douglas, 121–122
men
 changing expectations of, 6, 7,
  44–48
 lack of options for, 12
 rejection of FWAs by, 64–67
 work trade-offs by, 5
Mexico, 29
Microsoft, 31
MIT, 52, 80, 92
Moen, Phyllis, 32, 40, 61, 63
mommy track, 69
Morris, Hans, 42, 68
mothers
 bias against, 65–66
 caregiving responsibilities of,
  34
My M&M's, 79–80
MySpace, 177, 181

National Academy of Sciences,
  65–66
nontraditional households, 2,
  33–34

Ogilvy & Mather, 53, 87–89,
  118–20
1-800-Flowers, 52

one-off deals, 70
Open Work, 54–55
option value, 88–89, 171
organizational hierarchy, changes
    in, 1
organizations, benefits of MCC
    for, 9
outsourcing, rising, 6

Pace dimension, 91–92, 96, 97
paternity leave, 47–48
people-first strategy, 149
PepsiCo, 93
performance evaluations, 70–71,
    99, 163
performance hurdles, 101, 135
performance measures, Workload
    dimension and, 92–93
Perlow, Leslie, 176–177
Personal Pursuits program,
    158–159
Pfeffer, Jeffrey, 111
Piantidosi, Frank, 144
Piller, Frank, 80
Pitney Bowes, Inc., 93
Prince, Chuck, 42
Princeton University, 92
priorities, changing, 48–51, 86,
    102–105
professional degrees, percentage
    of awarded to women, 37–38
promotion goals, 137–38
promotion opportunities, FWAs
    and, 71–72
psychic benefit, 89. See also option
    value
Puget Sound Energy, 93

Quigley, Jim, 123

recruitment costs, 23, 182–183
remote-work arrangements,
    51–55, 153–154
Results-Oriented Work Environ-
    ment (ROWE), 94
retirement, delayed, 185
Richert, Eric, 54
Rodgers, Charles, 11–12
Roehling, Patricia, 32, 40, 63
Role dimension, 94–95, 96, 97
Ryan, Owen, 144

Salzberg, Barry, 127
Sandman, James J., 7, 72,
    116–117
SAS, 110–15
Schedule dimension. See
    Location/Schedule
    dimension
Schwartz, Felice N., 31
senior executives. See also
    managers
    lack of FWA opportunities for,
    68–69
Serwin, Kecia, 111–114
single-parent families, 33–34
60 Minutes, 74–75, 96
skepticism, conquering, 155–156
skilled labor, shrinking pool of, 6
Sloan Foundation, 93
social-networking technology,
    177, 180, 181
success, measuring, 164–165
success stories, 155–156

Sun Microsystems, 53–55
Sweet, Stephen, 61

talent management processes,
    integrating MCC into exist-
    ing, 98–102, 134–142,
    162–163
team-based work, 93, 131–132
technology
    impact of, 6, 51–55, 153–154,
    172
    social-networking, 177, 180,
    181
    virtual private networks, 52,
    177–179
tenure track, 92
text messaging, 51–52
thin-client applications, 52
time commitment, 161
TiVo revelation, 148–149
trade-offs
    from FWAs, 11–14, 71–72
    managing, 20–22
    work-life, 4–5, 7, 11–14
transparency, 8, 85, 86–87, 90,
    170, 180

U.S. workforce. See also workforce
    shrinking numbers in, 29
    statistics on, 6
University of California, Berkeley,
    92
University of California, Davis
    Graduate School of Manage-
    ment, 39
University of Southern California,
    170

value creation, 180–181
videoconferencing, 52, 174
Vinson and Elkins, 92
virtual offices, 51–55
virtual private networks, 52,
    177–179

Wackerbarth, Rick, 134–135, 136
Wall Street Journal, 79
Wharton Center of Leadership &
    Change Management, 41
Wikipedia, 180
Williams, Jon, 135, 136, 143
women
    biological clock, 40
    career-family issues faced by,
    4–5, 39–44
    in college, 37
    different career paths of, 39–44
    increasing numbers of, in work-
    force, 6–7, 36–44
    turnover rate for, 62
workers. See also employees
    knowledge, 27–31, 182–83
    shortage of skilled, 27–31
workforce
    changes in, 168
    diversity in, 1
    dual-career households, 2,
    33–34, 187–188
    foreign labor markets, 29–31
    increasing numbers of women
    in, 6–7, 36–44
    movement of women in and
    out of, 39–44
    shrinking numbers in, 28
Workforce Crisis (Dychtwald,
    Erickson, and Morison), 29

workforce trends, 5–7, 25–56
  brain drain, 152
  changing family structures,
    31–36
  changing male expectations,
    44–48
  convergence of, 26, 55–56
  expectations of Generations X
    and Y, 48–51
  increasing numbers of women,
    6–7, 36–44
  shortage of skilled workers,
    27–31
  technological changes, 51–55,
    172
  tying to day-to-day experiences,
    154–155
work-life balance, 2, 44, 46–47,
    59–61, 116–117, 187–188.
    See also career-life fit

work-life trade-offs, 4–5, 7,
    11–14
Workload dimension, 92–93, 96,
    97, 141
workplace
  challenges of tomorrow's,
    182–186
  evolution of, 172–82
  rethinking of traditional, 10
work priorities
  across generations, 48–51
  changing, 86, 102–5
work space reconfigurations,
    172–177
Worley, Christopher G., 170

YouTube, 177, 181
Yale Women Center, 41

ABOUT THE AUTHORS

A respected and accomplished advisor, **Cathleen Benko** is Deloitte's first Managing Principal of Talent, responsible for driving the organization's commitment to attract, develop, and advance a highly skilled and increasingly diverse workforce, which today comprises more than forty-thousand people.

Before assuming her current role, Cathy had dual responsibilities for leading Deloitte Consulting's high-technology industry sector as well as Deloitte's award-winning Women's Initiative. Previously, she was Deloitte Consulting's first Global e-Business Leader.

Cathy is coauthor of *Connecting the Dots: Aligning Projects and Objectives in Unpredictable Times* (Harvard Business School Press, 2003). In recognition of her professional skill and achievement, she has been named one of the "25 Most Influential Consultants" and a "Frontline Leader" by *Consulting Magazine*. She has been cited repeatedly for her accomplishments by a number of prestigious organizations, including Women in Technology International (WITI) and the *San Francisco Business Times*, which has named her one of the "Most Influential Women in the Bay Area" for six consecutive years.

Cathy earned her MBA from Harvard Business School and a Bachelor of Science degree from Ramapo College. She is a member of Deloitte's Executive Committee and the Deloitte Foundation Board. She lives in Northern California with her husband and two children.

As Senior Advisor to Deloitte's Women's Initiative (WIN), **Anne Weisberg** is responsible for designing and implementing the organization's national strategy for the retention and advancement of women. She is a recognized expert in the field of diversity, gender, and work/life integration.

Prior to joining Deloitte, Anne was a Senior Director in the Advisory Services practice at Catalyst, where she advised clients on diversity strategies. Anne directed a large-scale study of careers in the legal profession, *Women in Law: Making the Case* (Catalyst, 2001). She is also coauthor of *Everything a Working Mother Needs to Know* (Doubleday, 1994). Previously, Anne practiced law in New York and clerked for a federal judge in Chicago.

Anne received her JD cum laude from Harvard Law School and her Bachelor of Science degree Phi Beta Kappa from the University of California, Berkeley. She and her husband live in Manhattan and have five children between them.